THE RESPONSIBLE SELF

The Responsible Self

An Essay in Christian Moral Philosophy

H. Richard Niebuhr

Introduction by
James M. Gustafson

Foreword by
William Schweiker

Westminster John Knox Press
Louisville, Kenucky

Copyright © 1963 by Florence M. Niebuhr
Foreword © 1999 Westminster John Knox Press

First published by Harper & Row, Publishers, 1963

Library of Theological Ethics edition published by
Westminster John Knox Press 1999

This book is printed on acid-free paper that meets the American National Standards Institute Z39.48 standard. ∞

PRINTED IN THE UNITED STATES OF AMERICA

99 00 01 02 03 04 05 06 07 08 — 10 9 8 7 6 5 4 3 2 1

Library of Congress Cataloging-in-Publication Data

A catalog record for this book may be obtained from the Library of Congress.

ISBN 0-664-22152-1

CONTENTS

General Editors' Introduction   vii

Foreword by William Schweiker   ix

THE RESPONSIBLE SELF

Preface by Richard R. Niebuhr   1

Introduction by James M. Gustafson   6

Prologue: On Christian Moral Philosophy   42

1. The Meaning of Responsibility   47
2. Responsibility in Society   69
3. The Responsible Self in Time and History   90
4. Responsibility in Absolute Dependence   108
5. Responsibility in Sin and Salvation   127

Appendix   148

A. Metaphors and Morals   149
B. Responsibility and Christ   161

Index   179

LIBRARY OF THEOLOGICAL ETHICS

General Editors' Introduction

The field of theological ethics possesses in its literature an abundant inheritance concerning religious convictions and the moral life, critical issues, methods, and moral problems. The Library of Theological Ethics is designed to present a selection of important texts that would otherwise be unavailable for scholarly purposes and classroom use. The series engages the question of what it means to think theologically and ethically. It is offered in the conviction that sustained dialogue with our predecessors serves the interests of responsible contemporary reflection. Our more immediate aim in offering it, however, is to enable scholars and teachers to make more extensive use of classic texts as they train new generations of theologians, ethicists, and ministers.

The volumes included in the Library comprise a variety of types. Some make available English-language texts and translations that have fallen out of print; others present new translations of texts previously unavailable in English. Still others offer anthologies or collections of significant statements about problems and themes of special importance. We hope that each volume will encourage contemporary theological ethicists to remain in conversation with the rich and diverse heritage of their discipline.

ROBIN W. LOVIN
DOUGLAS F. OTTATI
WILLIAM SCHWEIKER

FOREWORD

The Responsible Self is a classic work in Christian ethics. It is one of a very select group of books that have decisively shaped Protestant and Roman Catholic ethics in the United States during the twentieth century. This is due, in good measure, to H. Richard Niebuhr's evocative way of defining moral theories in terms of conceptions of human existence. Against forms of ethics that picture human beings in terms of the act of making (Homo faber) or as citizens (Homo politicus), Niebuhr specifies a third picture, an ethics of responsibility. "What is implicit in the idea of responsibility," he wrote, "is the image of man-the-answerer, man engaged in dialogue, man in response to action upon him" (p. 56). We are Homo dialogicus. As Niebuhr examines these accounts of human existence, the reader is taken on a journey of self-understanding as well as inquiry into the meaning of Christian faith for the moral life. Little wonder that scholars, pastors, and students have found their way through the thicket of moral theory based on this scheme and its picture of human life.

There is irony in the fact that *The Responsible Self* is a classic of Christian ethics. Richard R. Niebuhr, the author's son, notes in the Preface that Niebuhr taught Christian ethics for some thirty years and yet had not produced a comprehensive statement. He died in 1962 while fashioning his ideas on ethics into a systematic work. The book before us is taken from his Robertson Lectures, given at the University of Glasgow in 1960. The Appendix also includes portions of his Earl Lectures, in which Niebuhr explored problems of moral and theological language as well as the role of Christ in an ethics of responsibility. Although *The Responsible Self* has become a classic in Christian ethics, the text is ironically not the author's intended form of presentation. This is the reason that the Introduction by James M. Gustafson is so important. Gustafson was a student and colleague of Niebuhr's and is also one of the foremost theological ethicists of his generation. Gustafson's Introduction sets this book within the flow of Niebuhr's thought and explores some of its distinctive claims. The reader is urged to consider the Preface and the Introduction as guides to the text.

While the Preface and Introduction lead the reader into the book, the purpose of this Foreword is to isolate the importance of *The Responsible Self* for some of the most pressing issues in current moral thought. Thus taken together, the Introduction, Preface, and Foreword will enable the reader to engage Niebuhr's thought with some sense of its origin, argument, and contemporary import. This should aid in the study and teaching of the text.

Several decades after it was written, how ought we to view *The Responsible Self* within the current task of theological ethics? One contribution of Niebuhr's work concerns the object of inquiry. The subtitle of this book is "An Essay in Christian Moral Philosophy." By this description Niebuhr meant to signal that his concern was not only with the beliefs and practices of the Christian community, although it certainly included that focus. The object of inquiry, as he puts it, was "human moral life in general." The book presents "the reflections of a Christian who seeks to understand the mode of his existence and that of his fellow beings as human agents" (p. 42). Christian belief with its focus on responsiveness to God in the whole of life can be used to aid in the analysis and understanding of moral existence. The task of Christian moral philosophy is nothing less than to interpret human life in all its depth and complexity.

Niebuhr's capacious and daring description of the enterprise of theological ethics is now suspect in many quarters. There are theologians who insist that the object of inquiry is not some ostensibly general human experience, but the unique mission and identity of the Christian community. Still other thinkers hold that claims about "human life" betray a false and insidious imposition of categories derived from the experience of some people (say, modern, Western males) onto others. The watchwords of the day are "particularity" and "identity," and this would seem to spell the end of Christian moral philosophy. However, that verdict cannot be easily sustained. It is true that all moral reflection is the work of particular persons situated in specific communities and traditions. Niebuhr saw this point and insisted upon it. Yet granting that fact does not mean that the object of moral inquiry is and must be limited to reflecting upon one's social and historical community. At some level every ethics makes claims about what it means to be a moral creature. Specific resources and beliefs can illuminate shared human concerns and problems. This is not imposition; it is inquiry aimed at understanding. One trajectory of thought prompted by Niebuhr's work is to define the object of moral inquiry in terms of pictures of human existence. To think otherwise is to constrict the scope of Christian moral inquiry.

Niebuhr's claim about the object of ethics is closely linked to another contribution of his work. In trying to understand and guide human life, we do so in light of some experience, activity, or purpose taken to be uniquely revealing of the meaning of existence. This is the point of Niebuhr's typology of moral theories. So-called teleological theories fasten on our capacities to shape the world and our own lives as basic to moral existence. What ends or ideals ought we to seek to realize? What kind of persons and communities should we strive to become? Behind these theories is a picture of human beings as "makers." Similarly, deontological theories focus on our lives in communities structured by laws, rules, and duties. What ought I to do? What are valid rules for social existence? What debt of justice do we owe others? The contention is that the moral character of human existence is disclosed in our lives as "citizens." Niebuhr held that persons are best defined by capacities of "responsiveness"; we answer to and with others. At issue in responsibility ethics (what he also called "cathecontic" ethics, which could be defined as "an ethic of appropriateness or fitting response") is how to respond "fittingly" within ongoing patterns and communities of interaction.

Niebuhr's focus on responsiveness resonates with contemporary debates about moral character or identity. Many thinkers, religious and nonreligious, rightly contend that we must begin moral reflection, not with the self and its aspirations and duties, but with the moral claim of others on the self. More generally stated, contemporary moral theory has shifted from the modern focus on the individual, autonomous acting person to explore moral identity within patterns of intersubjectivity and thus relationality. The constitutive fact of moral existence is not the self's encounter with itself, but our self-relation in and through encounters with others. Niebuhr, along with others of his generation, helped to move ethics beyond modern subjectivism. We always and only exist as selves in relationship to others, in relations characterized by responsible or irresponsible action. In this respect, the title of *The Responsible Self* is misleading. Niebuhr's focus is not on an isolated individual, but on a social self and social solidarity. We are, after all, Homo dialogicus.

However, Niebuhr's work calls for further reflection in terms of the formation of moral identity. While he escapes the trap of modern subjectivism, what remains unconsidered in his work, and, in fact, most responsibility ethics, is the discourse of virtue. Becoming responsible selves is a more arduous task than recognizing that human beings exist in relation to others. One must consider patterns of habituation and forces (social and individual) that form character. The recent revival of virtue theory, and thus reflection on the formation of character, can press cathecontic ethics to account for moral education and ideals of human excellence. Equally, the discourse of responsibility can revolutionize virtue theory by insisting on the "intersubjective" nature of human existence. Without the insight of responsibility ethics, virtue theory too easily can return to a focus on individual character, particular communities, and ideals of perfection outside of general patterns of interaction. Responsibility in relation to virtue theory is a topic that Christian moral philosophy must address.

The reader of *The Responsible Self* can follow trajectories of thought beyond the text in terms of current debates about the task of Christian ethics and also the nature and formation of moral identity. Yet Niebuhr's focus on human moral existence relates to still other issues in ethics. He argues that to be a moral being in community with others is to have some "center of value," a trust in and loyalty to something (a community, project, or ideal) that endows one's life and community with worth. Put abstractly, "value" and "agency" are intrinsically related ideas. If one removes the idea of value from an account of human beings, then the distinctiveness of persons as moral creatures is lost. This is a radical challenge to the many attempts in the natural and social sciences to define human beings from a value-neutral perspective. Niebuhr's work forecasts more recent developments in ethics by thinkers who insist that human beings are fundamentally valuing creatures. We always and necessarily live within some space or domain of worth and have to orient life in that context. Human communities and even perceptions of the world are saturated with value. This is basic to the intelligibility of existence.

On the question of value, some scholars have sensed a tension between Niebuhr's theology and ethics. Theologically he was committed to the idea of radical monotheism and hence affirming the reality of one ultimate center of value. His ethics, conversely, seems open to the positive import of the complex and diverse ways persons as valuing creatures shape their lives and world. This tension between religious monotheism and moral/cultural diversity can serve to provoke further reflection. One line of inquiry concerns pluralism. It is plainly the case that the ethicist of the twenty-first century must recognize the diversity of lives, cultures, traditions, and communities. Sensitive to the diversity of cultures and peoples, Niebuhr, theologically speaking, contrasted radical monotheistic faith with a polytheism of values he saw in Western societies. Christian existence is defined by one central value, and this fact challenges the many centers of value, the many "gods" of this world. He makes this argument in his book *Radical Monotheism and Western Culture*, also in the Library of Theological Ethics. The historical context of that book was the terror of world war and the virtual deification of states and their causes in war.

The Christian moral philosopher must continue to engage deeply the human importance of cultural values and moral pluralism. Yet the context of current thought is a spreading international market economy, advancing technology, and the global media system. The extension of human power through technology means that we can alter the natural environment and even the genetic structure of species. Additionally, cultural images flow in the media, shaping persons' conceptions of their lives and their world even as the diversity of human communities and moral outlooks is obvious. In other words, conceptions of human existence are deeply bound to cultural forces shaping how the world is pictured and human goodness understood. Engagement with the question of pluralism need not, and cannot, forestall the attempt in good faith to speak about shared human matters. If anything, our pluralistic age reveals the diversity of peoples and the interdependent character of the human adventure on this planet. These facts demand that the Christian moral philosopher release the vibrancy of tradition to provide orientation for living.

The reality of moral diversity in an age of globalization requires a subtle account of pluralism. In this respect, Niebuhr's construal of human beings as valuers might be his most fruitful contribution to current ethics and the challenge of pluralism. Yet one ought not dismiss the theme of radical monotheism. Niebuhr was not advocating a heteronomous vision of the divine or quickly judging other religious and moral outlooks. Indeed, the uniqueness of his religious vision for moral reflection has barely been grasped. By linking a dialogical picture of human beings with this claim about the irreducible connection between moral identity and some orienting value, Niebuhr was asserting within moral theory a point basic to his theology. This assertion is extremely important in our age. It signals another trajectory of thought at the interface of radical monotheism and responsibility ethics.

Niebuhr argued that two questions vex human existence. Is power good? Can goodness be powerful in history? We know all too well that the innocent suffer in this world; all too rarely does righteousness triumph. The ultimate forces of the vast universe seem impervious to our treasured ideas about human flourishing. Christian conviction, Niebuhr proclaimed, does not retreat from the facts of life nor despair about life's worth. In Jesus Christ one sees that the ultimate power of all reality (God) is good and that righteousness is not without its witness. Christian faith, Niebuhr liked to say following A. N. Whitehead, is a transition from encountering God as enemy to meeting God as Friend. It is a revolution in one's perception of the world and center of value. God the slayer is also God the creator and redeemer.

The Responsible Self provides the moral theory consistent with this religious vision. Trust in the one living God means morally that the power to act, to be an agent, is transformed to respond fittingly to the created worth of others. The responsible self or community apprehends others not as enemies but as fellow members of a comprehensive moral community as wide and deep as being itself. This is the force of Niebuhr's central claim about responsibility. "Responsibility affirms: 'God is acting in all actions upon you. So respond to all actions upon you as to respond to his action'" (p. 126). All of reality, every relation, is a context in which to respond to God, the ultimate source of value, the one in whom power and goodness are one. A contribution of Niebuhr's work, then, is to link a conception of value to moral identity in such a way as to counter moral skepticism and also the celebration of the will-to-power. Surely this moral vision is sorely needed in a time when hope easily flags and systems of economic, political, and technological power seem to rule.

Here then is the trajectory for further work in ethics. The Christian moral philosopher must enter debates not only about the object of ethics and moral character. She or he must also consider the reality of goodness, and this entails renewed engagement with moral naturalism and realism in ethics. The demand facing ethics in a postmodern age, I judge, is to provide an account of moral goodness not reducible to the celebration of power in order to protect and promote the fragility of finite existence. And this requires specifying the moral good in terms of real features of existence. Theologically considered, this is the moral meaning of Christian beliefs about the reality of the incarnation, creation, and Christ's love and suffering for others. These beliefs can shed surprising light on our moral situation, the status of the good, and the massive extension of human power in our age. They provide a way to understand and yet challenge the centrality of power in a technological, postmodern world.

One last contribution to ethics can be mentioned. Contemporary ethics is beset with endless debates about the possibility and necessity of validating a moral outlook. Some thinkers are critical of modern Western moral theory and its aspiration to universality and objectivity. They insist that moral rationality is tradition constituted. The truth of a moral vision arises from its relation to a living tradition and the capacity to address particular features of life. Other ethicists counter these arguments and insist that moral truth requires public validation. Moral rationality exceeds the limits of our specific traditions. Niebuhr eschews the debate between universalists and particularists. He spoke of his work as "confessional," by which he meant working with the resources of a community to see what light they might cast on life. This is one reason why he took metaphor, symbol, and narrative so seriously, thereby helping to forward the recent attention to these topics in theology and ethics.

From Niebuhr's perspective, moral and theological reflection demonstrates its validity by its pragmatic capacity to illuminate our lot and life. One should not expect universal agreement on moral principles without a deep engagement with the forms of life, discourse, and beliefs surrounding and undergirding those principles. Yet in the same way, the validity of a moral outlook is not defined merely internally to a community's discourse and practice. If the universalist fails to grasp that responsibility is always a matter of actions and relations in specific times and places, then the particularist has not seen that responsibility entails participation in a moral community that exceeds limited communities.

Niebuhr's ideas about confessional theology as well as symbol, metaphor, and narrative are open to further reflection about moral rationality, truth, and interpretation. Just as responsibility ethics needs to engage work in virtue theory, ideas about pluralism, and moral realism, so too it can and ought to engage in current debates within hermeneutics about the shape of human understanding. Still, Niebuhr's stance on the question of the status of moral claims is promising. The only way to "validate" an ethics is to show the capacity of one's own community's discourse to illuminate and guide our lives as moral beings. In a word, to specify the truth of Christian faith means engaging in the daring enterprise called Christian moral philosophy.

The Responsible Self insightfully addresses topics that are still important in moral philosophy. I have argued that one can trace trajectories of thought from this book to current concerns about the object of moral inquiry, conceptions of agency, pluralism, ideas about power and goodness, and how one can and ought to show the truth of an ethics. On each of these topics further work needs to be done. Yet as important as these contributions and trajectories are, the tenor of Niebuhr's work may be of greater significance for theological ethics. Niebuhr boldly insisted that the deepest questions of human life are at once moral and also religious. At stake in ethics, finally, is how persons and communities can and ought to respond to God in order fittingly to direct their lives and power. The clarity of this insight and the precision of Niebuhr's expression of it lend compelling force to the pages of this work. Now, in the Library of Theological Ethics, this classic work is available to a new generation of scholars, pastors, and students.

WILLIAM SCHWEIKER

THE RESPONSIBLE SELF

PREFACE

AT THE TIME H. Richard Niebuhr died in July, 1962, he was
at work fashioning into book form the basic ideas and constructive and critical principles of the systematic Christian ethics that
he had taught and reflected upon during more than thirty years,
for the most part at the Yale Divinity School. While all of his
books, from the time of *The Social Sources of Denominationalism*
onward, bespeak themes and problems that were integral to his
heart and mind, none of them directly incorporates the fundamen·
tal architectonic ideas of the discipline of systematic ethics into
which he had poured the largest part of his energies. If (to borrow
an image from the following pages) we mortals were free to regard
our lives as works of art or at least as providing the raw materials
from which we could shape a completed building, then many of
us would have wished that the author of this volume might have
been given time to put in place the stone that is the key, as it

1

were, to the span of his lifelong intellectual endeavors. As it is, however, the greater part of his ethics must remain simply in the form of his own lecture notes and the transcripts of his lectures that students took with them from the classroom. That this is the case is due principally to the fact that my father always feared once he put his ideas into print, the possibility of reinterpreting and re-thinking them in the classroom would vanish, and instead of being a dialogue with his students, his colleagues, and with the times at large his ethical reflections would become a finished piece of busi-ness, a part of the past rather than a lively, appreciative, and critical response to the present. The kind of closed thinking that can create the semblance of motion only by adding further scholia and specific applications of fixed and irrevocable definitions and axioms was as distasteful to him as the closed and parochial societies that abound in the worlds of academics and religion as much as in other human realms. I do not mean to imply that the basic convictions of his mind were forever shifting and altering, for there is a clear consistency in his thought throughout his entire career of teaching and writing, but he was continually engaged in thinking through his convictions and principles from new angles of vision and in the light of new insights caught from his reading and association with the authors of volumes in philosophy, history, psychology, soci-ology, philosophy of science and aesthetics. This endeavor always to find new approaches for his own work in ethics is exemplified in the discussion of metaphors and morals that stands at the be-ginning of *The Responsible Self* and in the appendix. It would be only his most recent students at Yale who heard and watched him reflect in this vein upon his central theme of the ethics of responsibility.

For these reasons, he deferred the writing of his ethics until the time of his retirement, and since he did not live to enjoy that retirement, for these same reasons we have so little of his ethics in published form.

Upon his desk at the time of his death I found the drafts of two chapters intended for *The Responsible Self,* constituting greatly expanded versions of portions of the substance of the following pages, as well as numerous sketches and outlines of various projections of his ethics for publication. It would be exceedingly difficult to conjecture from these evidences what he conceived the final shape of his publication program to be, in the last weeks of his life. One thing is certain, however, and that is that the book or books would have constituted a thorough reworking of his Yale classroom lectures, and, as James Gustafson points out in his introduction, former students will recognize much that is familiar in these chapters, but they will also find that some of the author's pivotal theological ideas appear only indirectly or in the background, for they had been relegated to fuller exposition at other points lying outside of the scope of the present volume. It is the editors' and publisher's hope, however, that some of these deficiencies can be partially remedied in the projected volume of H. Richard Niebuhr's essays, sermons, and other literary remains that is to follow.

The Responsible Self in the form in which it is here published is taken directly from the Robertson Lectures that H. Richard Niebuhr delivered at the University of Glasgow in the Spring of 1960. Some of this material was also presented, though in altered form and with omissions and supplementations, as the Earl Lectures at the Pacific School of Religion and in a series of addresses at The Riverside Church in New York City, a series cut short by illness in the Winter of 1962. The appendix in the present volume incorporates portions of these Earl Lectures.

The style which the reader will encounter here, therefore, is that of the formal lecture, unencumbered for the most part by citations and references to other contemporary works in theological and philosophical ethics and, on the other hand, unaccompanied by the spontaneous asides and illustrations that marked his less formal presentations in his Yale classroom. Hence this volume displays neither the polish and chiseled qualities that would have marked it had the author himself prepared it for the press, nor the degree of openness and free play of thought that the classroom permits and elicited from him. However, what appears here is still unmistakably the work of his hand, and it is our hope that what the reader finds here will be no less edifying and stimulating to his own thinking than the completed *magnum opus* would have been.

At the outset of his lectures in Glasgow, H. Richard Niebuhr, acknowledging the honor that had been bestowed upon him by the invitation of the University, continued his introduction in the following words: "But I am more aware of the challenge issued than of the honor bestowed. Lectureships, such as this one, particularly at the universities of Scotland and England, play a peculiar role in the life of scholarship and teaching. They challenge men who have spent their years in classrooms and studies to bring together in well-considered unity the ideas with which they have been working, and to make available in concentrated form, as it were, the consequences of their labors. . . . I shall attempt to present to you in these lectures a summation and an ordering of some of the reflections on the moral life that have developed in my mind during a long period of teaching in the field of Christian ethics. In what I shall set before you in the way of an analysis of the responsibility of selfhood I shall be dealing not with the subject of Christian ethics proper but with an introduction to that subject. I am afraid that these reflections fall under a heading, suspected and rejected by philosophy and theology alike in our time—that hybrid thing sometimes called Christian philosophy. But by whatever name it is called, it represents the effort of faith to understand itself. Its motto is: *Fides quaerens intellectum,* or, since the understanding of faith that is presupposed is Protestant, *Fiducia* or *Fidelitas quaerens intellectum.*

The family of the author and the editors of this book wish to thank particularly the University of Glasgow for its invitation to H. Richard Niebuhr, which has ultimately led to the publication of these Robertson Lectures, and the Pacific School of Religion likewise, where the Earl Lectures were delivered; also to Charles Scribner's Sons for permission to quote, on pages 113f. below, from the essay, "Ultimate Religion," in the volume *Obiter Scripta, Lectures, Essays and Reviews,* by George Santayana, edited by Justus Buchler and Benjamin Schwartz (copyright 1936 by Charles Scribner's Sons); also to Alfred A. Knopf, Inc. for permission to quote from Eunice Tietjens' *Body and Raiment* (copyright 1919 by Alfred A. Knopf, Inc.) on page 137 below. In addition, it would be less than just to our own sentiments not to express our gratitude to Eugene Exman and Melvin Arnold for their encouragement, solid support, and more than willing readiness to bring this book into print.

RICHARD R. NIEBUHR

INTRODUCTION

by James M. Gustafson

"THE RESPONSIBLE SELF" is an integrating and persistent theme in the ethical thought and teaching of H. Richard Niebuhr. In any presentation of his lifelong reflections that he would have made, it would necessarily be central. The theme provided him an opportunity to be a philosopher of the Christian moral life, rather than a moral theologian who primarily explicated Biblical foundations of Christian behavior, or one who derived all his knowledge of Christian morality from theological dogmas. Thus by attending to this theme for the lectures presented in this book, he has revealed his basic procedure of Christian ethical thought, and incorporated a surprisingly large section of the material that constituted his lecture course in Christian ethics at Yale Divinity School over three decades.

Yet students of H. Richard Niebuhr will not find this book to include a particular block of the course material as he gave it. This is so for two major reasons. In the first place, he conscientiously reworked the lecture material for each presentation of the course, giving it different outlines from time to time, developing new patterns of ideas as he worked through things he had thought about before, reflecting upon what he said in relation to books recently read or schools of thought emerging on the intellectual horizon. He disliked the possibility of thinking his own thoughts after himself, and thus never fell into a rutted way of delivering his major set of lectures. Thus, because of its changing characteristics, no single presentation of his own thought would exactly duplicate what students in any one generation heard.

In the second place, his design for the lecture series that issue in this book led him to bring the theme of the responsible self into sharp focus, but at the same time to relate it in an integrated way to many other features of his thought. He debated in his own mind whether he ought to publish his systematic Christian ethics as a single large book, or as two or three separate books. These Robertson Lectures constitute an approach to his systematic thought through the theme of their title. Another approach would probably have been made through the more distinctively theological elements of his ethics—response to God, the Creator, Governor, and Redeemer. The finely woven character of his systematic ethics made it necessary to bring into the picture those elements of his thought that are peripheral to any particular theme. Thus, while the present book is derived most heavily from what he often lectured on under the rubric of "The Structure and Dynamics of the Moral Life," he has brought into it elements of his view of the relation of philosophical to theological ethics, his typology of ethics as teleological, deontological, and "response ethics," his thoughts on law and gospel, on sin and redemption, and many other topics. There are even a few indications of the specific interpretations of man's moral experience in race, or family, or politics, that might have constituted yet another thematic approach into the systematic thought. Those readers who are familiar with his thinking here will find many elements of it drawn together in relation to the theme of the responsible self in a way that they have not seen or heard before.

The present book is true to his basic approach to ethics. He conceived of Christian ethics to be the effort of the Christian community to criticize its moral action by means of reflection. This critical inquiry is not confined to the process of moral self-judgment in the community, to the process of evaluation of its life in the light of certain expectations and norms. Rather it is a critical inquiry in a more generous philosophical sense, an inquiry into the nature of its moral life, the principles of its life (principles in terms of those things that are most universally true and proper about its being). Thus a major part of ethics is a phenomenological analysis of man's moral existence. For H. Richard Niebuhr this involved more than a behavioral description of the visible, audible, historically manifest morals of Christians. Ethics is not the narrative account of the moral action of members of the Christian community. It has the task of disclosing the basic pattern, the morphology of the life and action of the Christian community in the moral sphere—the way of thinking and acting that is true to its character as a community of men before God. Hence it is not surprising to find more references to philosophers than to theologians in his development of the theme "The Responsible Self," for his own constructive effort to depict the nature of Christian ethics has a major common referent with theirs—namely, the universal phenomenon of human morality and reflection upon it. What he has written, then, contributes not only to a theological discussion about ethics, but also to the broader human discussion.

At the same time he is interested in the moral action of the historic Christian community. This means that its own particular pattern of interpretation of moral life receives attention—life in the church, life in relation to the One God, life in relation to the

Son Jesus Christ, life in sin and in reconciliation. But in this book these particular religious themes are addressed through the more universal moral theme of responsibility. Thus the substantive discussion of what he often lectured on under the rubric of "The Principles of Christian Action" is more alluded to and suggested than it is thoroughly explicated. Those readers who have heard him expound these themes may find the present book to be an attenuated exposition of what they remember. Those who have not heard him expound these themes might be prone to assume that he failed to come to grips with the major themes of the Christian community's faith.

It is the purpose of this introductory essay to indicate some elements in Niebuhr's thought that are not brought into the present book, and to develop a bit more fully some elements that are only briefly dealt with. No one can ever think the thoughts after his teacher who tried not to think his own thoughts after himself. The present book does not contain materials that would naturally have appeared in a second volume, dealing with "The Principles of Christian Action," and a third, "Christian Responsibility in Common Life," dealing with the interpretation of marriage and the family, politics and economics, war and international relations in the light of the idea of responsibility and of the theological principles. These we cannot have from his own pen. It is my lamented responsibility to try to indicate, for the readers of this volume, how the theme of "The Responsible Self" is related to other aspects of H. Richard Niebuhr's more inclusive systematic thought on Christian ethics.

THE SETTING FOR "THE RESPONSIBLE SELF"

The reader who is acquainted with some of H. Richard Niebuhr's previously published books and essays can provide part of the setting for this book. In *Christ and Culture*,[1] for example, one

[1] New York: Harper & Row, 1951.

finds not only an illuminating typology of Christian ethics with reference to the theme of the title, but also in the first and last chapters particularly important clues to Niebuhr's understanding of the function and the field of Christian ethics. One finds there the priority of thinking in terms of relationships—man to God, and man to man before God—that is expressed in this book. One finds a statement of the necessity of speaking about ethics in relation to a particular religious and historical standpoint. There is a simple statement of his relational value-theory—"worth is worth in relation to God" (p. 18). He sets forth the place of love within faith and hope and in terms of the love of God. He briefly describes the meaning of "Relativism in Faith" and of his "Social Existentialism." All of these elements appear again in the present book, in a somewhat different form.

In *Radical Monotheism and Western Culture*[2] he gave us his most extensive exposition of how to think and to live in terms of the relative authority of all human and cultural forms, while acknowledging them to be under the sovereignty of the One God. Included in that book is one particular essay that is indispensable for a more technical understanding of Niebuhr's ethics, namely, "The Center of Value," in which he develops his relational or social theory of value. In a response to a critique of an earlier version of that essay he discloses something of his own intellectual self-understanding in the sphere of ethics. "Philosophically, it is more indebted to G. H. Mead than to Aristotle; theologically, it is closer, I believe, to Jonathan Edwards ('consent of being to being') than to Thomas Aquinas." The present book is impregnated with this American standpoint, more fully disclosed in the essays of *Radical Monotheism*.

The Purpose of the Church and Its Ministry[3] provides the reader another occasion in which to see the basic thought pattern reflected

[2] New York: Harper & Row, 1960.
[3] New York: Harper & Row, 1956.

in "The Responsible Self." In the first chapter of that book, he gives an account of the church, of its purpose ("The Increase of Love of God and Neighbor"), and of how the church ought to think about its purposes, that reveals the fruitfulness of his sophisticated, more technical reflections on the nature of the Christian life. Without using the more academic terms "triadic pattern of relationships," "relativism in faith," "consent of being to being," etc., he gives one of the most persuasive interpretations of the meaning of love in recent Christian literature, and suggests again the importance of making distinctions between proximate and ultimate goals and purposes. And one needs to turn back to *The Meaning of Revelation*[4] for a fuller interpretation of Niebuhr's view of how God is known and how man is known in the knowledge of God. The person who reads that book carefully and sympathetically is better prepared to understand the way of thought in this book, as well as to catch many nuances in its text. In addition to these books, there are also a number of key articles in various publications which enable the reader to comprehend more fully the intellectual setting of the present lectures.[5]

[4] New York: The Macmillan Company, 1941.
[5] The following are particularly important for Niebuhr's ethical thought: "Value Theory and Theology," in *The Nature of Religious Experience*, eds. J. S. Bixler, R. L. Calhoun, and H. R. Niebuhr (New York: Harper & Row, 1937); "The Responsibility of the Church for Society," in *The Gospel, the Church and the World*, ed. K. S. Latourette (New York: Harper & Row, 1946); "Evangelical and Protestant Ethics," in *The Heritage of the Reformation*, ed. E. J. F. Arndt (New York: Richard R. Smith, 1950); "Biblical Ethics" and his introductions to other writings in Beach and Niebuhr, *Christian Ethics* (New York: Ronald Press, 1955); "Towards a New Otherworldliness," in *Theology Today*, I (1944), pp. 78–87; "The Ego-Alter Dialectic and the Conscience," in *Journal of Philosophy*, XLII (1945), pp. 352–359; "The Triad of Faith," in *Andover Newton Bulletin*, XLVII (1954), pp. 3–12; and "The Idea of Covenant and American Democracy," in *Church History*, XXIII (1954), pp. 126–135. For critical and interpretative studies of Niebuhr's thought, see *Faith and Ethics, The Theology of H. Richard Niebuhr*, ed. Paul Ramsey (New York: Harper & Row, 1957).

Even the reader who is well acquainted with Niebuhr's previous publications will be provoked to raise certain questions pertaining to the present book. It is not my intention to raise them for the reader and thus to underestimate his intelligence. There are, however, three aspects of the systematic ethics which might especially aid the reader better to understand the setting of the present book. One is an answer to the question: "What is the usefulness of Christian ethics done in this critical analytic mode?" A second is: "What is the place of Scripture in the elaboration of human responsibility before God?" The third is: "In responding to God's action in all the actions upon us in our historical experience, how do we see God disclose himself to us?"

USES OF ETHICS

What are we to expect from the study of ethics, particularly as the critical inquiry addressed to the nature of moral action? What are we to hope for from the work of the moral theologian? Dietrich Bonhoeffer has given a valuable limitation to what the moral theologian can do for us in his *Ethics,* one which is quoted with enthusiasm by Karl Barth:

"An ethic cannot be a book in which there is set out how everything in the world actually ought to be but unfortunately is not, and an ethicist cannot be a man who always knows better than others what is to be done and how it is to be done. An ethic cannot be a work of reference for moral action which is guaranteed to be unexceptionable, and the ethicist cannot be the competent critic and judge of every human activity. An ethic cannot be a

---

The essays in that volume by Paul Ramsey, George Schrader, Julian Hartt, Waldo Beach, and James Gustafson all relate to Niebuhr's ethics. One of Professor Niebuhr's former students wrote a book which contains a summary interpretation of aspects of Niebuhr's Christian ethics. It is E. Clinton Gardner, *Biblical Faith and Social Ethics* (New York: Harper & Row, 1960), especially portions of Chaps. 5 and 7.

retort in which ethical or Christian human beings are produced, and the ethicist cannot be the embodiment or ideal type of a life which is, on principle, moral."[6]

H. Richard Niebuhr was by no means happy with the theological ground that supported Bonhoeffer's *Ethics* (or Barth's either, for that matter) and sought a much larger place for critical reflection about the action of Christians than is present in either Barth or Bonhoeffer. But he was clear about what could and could not be expected from ethics as an intellectual discipline in a manner not foreign to Bonhoeffer's assertion. For example, some readers of this book may look for some prescriptive definition about how a responsible self ought to behave in one particular instance or another, or they might look for some rules of responsible behavior, or for some assurance that the Christian community is by definition of its existence in Christ a community of superior responsibility. These things he will not find. This is no manual with an immediate practicality in determining for others what their moral life ought to be. Niebuhr's firm conviction that ethics could not provide such was well-grounded.

One cannot expect from Niebuhr's ethics a set of close definitions of universally appropriate behavior, or even of occasional behavior. The task of the critical inquirer into the moral life precedes any such regulative prescriptions. His task is to analyze "ethos," to lay bare the roots and fundamental character of a community's moral life. Out of this discourse in the community can come an understanding of what ought to be done, but it is never the moral theologian's prerogative to be the moral dictator, and even his function as guide or counselor is to be understood in a very special way. Why is this the case?

There is no proof that the morals of the Christian community

---

[6] D. Bonhoeffer, *Ethics* (London: SCM Press, 1955), p. 236; quoted by Barth, *Church Dogmatics*, III/4 (Edinburgh: T. and T. Clark, 1961), p. 10.

are finally any better than those of other communities, or even that the basic principles of the community are better. Niebuhr viewed with an element of indignation those efforts of moral theologians to claim and demonstrate the superiority of Christian ethics over other patterns, or to claim a self-sufficiency for Christian ethics—seeking to derive all moral wisdom from the Bible or from Jesus Christ alone, for example. Such efforts finally appear to be defensive, or to be falsely aggrandizing credit to the Christian community. The judgment of moral superiority of the Christian over the non-Christian, or of a Christian ethics over Aristotelian ethics, is up to God. The proper stance of the Christian community in its ethical reflection is self-criticism and repentance, not pride and aggrandizement.

Christian ethics starts with Christian beliefs. Something of the argument of Niebuhr's *Meaning of Revelation* is behind both what he claims for Christian ethics and how he limits the claims of Christian ethics. We cannot think ethically outside of Christian affirmations, but also we cannot claim thereby that they are demonstrably superior to all other affirmations. The Christian community cannot claim a superiority for its moral knowledge, or for its capacities to cultivate moral wisdom, or for its power to determine for others what the proper course of their affairs ought to be. Its uniqueness is that of its historical revelation of God, which the community confesses. Just as efforts in theology to assert or prove some absolute superiority of this revelation to other assertions about the knowledge of God are mistaken, so comparable efforts on the part of moral theologians are mistaken. The task of ethics is more the task of "digging" (to use a term F. D. Maurice loved, and Niebuhr appreciated because he found Maurice's stance toward his work to be a congenial one) than it is a task of constructing superior Christian human plans for God's activity. The prior question is "What is going on?" "What is God doing?" It is not "What should we do?"

If Niebuhr refuses to take us off the hooks of personal responsibility by prescribing our behavior for us, or by assuring us that we have the best morality in the world because it is Christian, is there any utility to his enterprise, or is he simply enjoying the contemplative intellectual life? He could hardly propose the study of ethics to have some value in and of itself, for his own value-theory suggests that things worthy of doing are worthy in part by virtue of their value to men. What then are the positive uses of ethical reflection?

Certainly the sympathetic reader will find some of the answers to this question in the effects of the present book. One value that Niebuhr found in, and claimed for, ethics, is the aid to self-knowledge. Ethics is not merely self-knowledge, any more than faith is merely self-knowledge, but self-knowledge is an important task of ethical inquiry and reflection. Here we have a theme that is currently familiar in existentialist views of the utility of the intellectual and religious enterprise. Niebuhr had a critical sympathy for such affirmations in this regard, but he did not hesitate to call upon Socrates as well, to indicate that there is a propriety in moving from the question "What is real?" to the question "Who am I?" When we ask about responsibility we are asking about ourselves. For the Christian, in the fashion of Calvin, this self-knowledge occurs *in relation to* the knowledge of God; for Niebuhr the substance of self-knowledge *is not derived out of* our knowledge of God as it appears to be with Barth.[7] Ethics is knowledge of

---

[7] This book makes perfectly clear how foreign Barth's pattern of theological thinking is to Niebuhr's. It becomes obvious in Niebuhr's Prologue and throughout the text that he is not attempting to derive an anthropology out of a Christology, or even out of Scripture alone. Another theological perspective Niebuhr criticized is reflected in W. Elert's claim: "The basic difference lies in the fact that theological ethics judges human quality exclusively by God's standards and looks at man as God sees him, while in content and method philosophical ethics is man's understanding of himself." *The Christian Ethos* (Philadelphia: Muhlenberg Press, 1957), p. 7.

ourselves in relation to our knowledge of God. And self-knowledge is no mere luxury to be cultivated during idle moments; it is essential to the responsible life. Its relation to the responsible life is not such that we can derive from our statements about ourselves further statements about what we are always to do; Niebuhr does not set out a body of propositions about the essential nature of man, and from that body of propositions formulate another one pertaining to what we ought to do. Self-knowledge affects our moral life in more complicated and subtle ways.

A related consequence of ethical analysis has been enumerated by Niebuhr, namely, its aid to men in their struggle to achieve integrity. The personal situation of the moral man always involves an effort to come to wholeness and orderliness in life. Men are always faced with recognition of the good, and yet their inability to do it; with the claims of family, church, and other groups upon them, and yet their aspiration to individuality; with the needs and desires of the body, and yet their moral self-consciousness that is not always in accord with these. Reflection on the moral life can help men to achieve a unity, a first loyalty, a center of personal integrity. It does this by aiding us to analyze the variety of commands we hear, the conflicts of values in which we are engaged, and the relativity of all values in relation to the one ultimate Good. It aids us in our decisions about the relations of values to each other, about the course of our active life. The aid to integrity in our moral and personal existence is not a primary purpose of ethical thought, but it is an important consequence of it.

Another way in which H. Richard Niebuhr described the importance of ethics was as an "aid in accuracy in action." In this book he refers to the importance of *hamartia,* of "missing the mark," as one aspect of our moral predicament. This notion fits nicely into the whole "response ethic" developed by Niebuhr. At this juncture it suggests that ethics cannot guarantee that one will always hit the mark, but it is an aid to accuracy. Proper ethical reflection in a democratic society will not enable men necessarily and easily to achieve the goal of equal rights for all citizens, for example, but it can help men direct their actions by that goal. It helps to avoid certain confusions that are bound to occur in our moral action—for example, the confusion of subjective qualities in life (love as a virtue) with objective values (love as an objective good). It demonstrates for us some of the fallacies that are often involved in our practical reason—particularly the oversimplifications pertaining to the goals and course of action that we are likely to make without careful reflection. It reveals some of our rationalizations and platitudes to us. Some of the tensions and conflicts in the moral life of a community that ethics helps to depict are not easily reconcilable, if they are reconcilable at all. Ethical inquiry does not dissolve discrepancies of purpose, nor does it determine proper procedures of action. But it enables men to have some objectification of their moral world, inner and outer, and thus contributes to the effectiveness of their action by clarifying their understanding of it.

The struggle for coherence and accuracy is both personal and social. Niebuhr often cited Walter Lippmann's use of a quotation from Aristophanes to open his analysis of "The Dissolution of the Ancestral Order," in *A Preface to Morals:* "Whirl is King, having driven out Zeus." Not only does the self struggle for integrity, but the society of which it is a part is a fragmented one, with loyalties and values that lead it in various directions at the same time. The devotion to truth in the scientific community may cause it to lose sight of the morally dubious uses to which scientific truth may be put in the social order. Devotion to beauty in itself may not be easily brought into relationship to the artist's vocation to be an interpreter of existence. The business community might well be so preoccupied with the values of efficiency and productivity that it loses sight of the values of truth and beauty. The religious community might become so valiant in pursuit of its inner and institutional life that it seems to claim God exclusively for itself as its independent province. In a sense, universities are a microcosm of the lack of social coherence in modern society, with their divergent purposes and perspectives that compete within them. Ethics, as an intellectual enterprise, enables us to bring more clarity into our interpretation of the social world of which we are a part—not by pure sociological analysis, but by ethical analysis, an analysis of values, goals, purposes, moral claims, and aspirations that compete, conflict, or co-exist uncomfortably. It does not give us an unequivocal rank-order of values to be sought in some universal order of preference to each other. It does not plot out the design for the ideal society in which all the tensions and ambiguities of social and moral incoherence are brought into a harmonious, beautiful whole. Rather, it clarifies our understanding of moral existence through its analysis and in turn enables us to be more responsible selves in the social world.

For Niebuhr, then, it is perhaps more accurate to speak of an indirect effect of ethical analysis upon moral life and action, than of an immediate and direct one. Ethics helps us to understand ourselves as responsible beings, our world as the place in which the responsible existence of the human community is exercised. Its practical utility is in its clarification, its interpretation, its provision of a pattern of meaning and understanding in the light of which human action can be more responsible. To some readers, this may appear to be something different from what they wish for and expect from ethics. It does not relieve them of personal responsibility to exercise their freedom, their capacity for judgment and action in the world. But each man is not left to himself alone, though each is personally responsible. The intellectual work of ethics, like the moral life described in this book, always takes place in community; it is a dialogue with others present to the thinking man. Thus communication with others is a part of the work of ethics itself. It is in this process of communication that the understanding of the world in its moral nature has its effect upon the moral outlook and actions of particular persons. It is through the action of persons that it affects the social world.

THE PLACE OF SCRIPTURE IN CHRISTIAN ETHICS

What is the place of the Bible in the critical analysis of the moral life of the Christian community? The present book contains no specific answer to this question. Niebuhr has answered it in part in *Christ and Culture,* particularly in Chapter 1, but the reader might be aided by an effort to deal with it directly out of his teaching. In his "Introduction to Biblical Ethics" (Beach and Niebuhr, *Christian Ethics*), he gave some of his views. For contemporary discussion, which is often so Biblically centered in ethics as well as in theology, it is important to bring out Niebuhr's reflections not only on the general problem, but also on the way in which Scripture informs the actual exposition of the principles of Christian action.

Niebuhr's general approach to the issue of Biblical authority in Christian ethics can be distinguished from two forms of "Biblicism." The first is the Biblicism of the Christian ethics of liberal theology, in which the basic foundation for ethical thought and teaching was to be found in the teachings of Jesus. There was a tendency in the liberal tradition to confine the significance of Scripture for ethics to these teachings, or at most to add to them certain statements of the Old Testament prophets. In contrast to this, Niebuhr participated in the recovery of the theological importance of the Bible and thus would not limit the Biblical authority for ethics to statements in the Bible that dealt with morals.

His appreciation for the recovery of the importance of Scripture, however, did not lead to what to him was a newer form of Biblicism. This second form is that in which the Bible becomes too exclusively the source of knowledge for man's ethical responsibility, and in which men feel prone to find the Biblical theological foundations for every serious moral act or thought. Niebuhr had little patience for efforts on the part of contemporary European theologians to try to solve the questions of the authority of the state, for example, by reworking Romans 13:1-7, or by finding in the Christological texts of Ephesians and Colossians the ground for ethical-theological interpretations of the nature of the human world. He was never convinced that as much moral wisdom was forthcoming from the Bible alone as theologians who had some morally wise things to say thought they were getting from the Bible. His openness to knowledge of man and the moral world not only from philosophy but also from the psychological and social sciences was great. Furthermore, he was acutely aware of the contemporary cultural situation in which the Biblical idiom in itself simply does not communicate what is ethically important about the Bible. Thus, among recent writers in Christian ethics, he found that Barth, Bonhoeffer, Otto Piper, Elert, and other European Lutherans tended to seek to be too exclusively Biblical, or Biblical theological (through appropriate Reformation eyes), really to address the complexities of the nature of human responsibility. The absence of frequent mention of this literature in the present book indicates that above all at the crucial point of understanding the nature of moral existence, he found more insight in philosophical writings. He had ready appreciation for the efforts of Helmut Thielicke to extend and expand the kinds of material that one had to bring into Christian ethics.[8] But he was confident enough in his own less Biblicistic approach to engage in his way of work without always seeking to defend it against potential criticism from theological colleagues; indeed he relished a freedom which he found in the American theological scene to be deeply involved in what the Scripture is saying to us without being bound to ground everything he wished to say in it.

[8] See, for example, *Theologische Ethik,* I (Tübingen: J. C. B. Mohr [Paul Siebeck], 1958), pp. 62 ff.

But as a moral theologian Niebuhr did not play fast and loose with the Bible. For the Christian it has a commanding authority. Within the Bible itself, which depicts the life of the human community before God, Scripture has authority, and in part a problematic authority. In the Old Testament there is the authoritative law, but one also finds the prophets with their living word, a word not grounded in the written word exclusively. The record of Jesus' own teaching is double-sided in this respect. On the one hand he uses the authority of the book—"till heaven and earth pass away, not an iota, not a dot, will pass from the law until all is accomplished." Yet in the same collection of sayings, the Sermon on the Mount, Jesus introduces another authority—"You have heard . . . But *I say* to you . . ." And even St. Paul, for whom the Christian's life is grounded in his direct participation in the Risen Lord and thus is free, relies upon Scriptural authority. The Christian moral theologian inescapably must take Scripture seriously, for the Bible itself takes it seriously.

But one cannot address the question in quantitative terms; one cannot properly ask: "How much authority does Scripture have?" In the task of Christian ethics in our time the question is seen differently from some other times. We find the Bible to be important not only in the moral teachings of Jesus, but in the Prophets, in the idea of a covenanted people, in the theology and ethical teachings of Paul and the Johannine literature. We read the Bible together with our knowledge of the ethical tradition of the Christian community—the tradition has authority along with Scripture. We read our Augustine, Calvin, Luther, Wesley, Edwards, F. D. Maurice, and our contemporaries. In this process Biblical and theological themes come into our view that are not obviously moral. We consider eschatology—the meaning of judgment, of resurrection, of the end, and what the life of a community is when it views history as a time of great expectation, as a place in which to pre-enact what the community believes the future to hold. We consider anthropology—what it is for man to be sinner, and what it is to be in God's grace. The particular moral teachings of Jesus, and of others in the New Testament, are to be seen in the wider Biblical framework.

Readers of *Radical Monotheism* are acquainted with Niebuhr's strong affirmations that only One is absolute, and all other beings, purposes, cultural expressions, politics, and religion are relative to Him. It is in this framework that he suggests the limitations of the authority of Scripture, and this is the framework out of which his irritation with Biblicism came. Since there is only one Absolute Power and Authority (authority, he often said, is the kind of power that is exercised over us by consent, and voluntarily negated by dissent), one cannot assign absolute authority to the Scripture. Its authority is a "mediate derived authority." The Church's moral life is not the only instance of such mediate authorities in human experience. In science and politics as well, there is a pluralism of authorities, none of which becomes the exclusive source of knowledge and insight. As in other communities, so in the church an authority can be unique without being exclusive. The Bible has such a status: it cannot be reduplicated elsewhere; in no other place is Jesus Christ presented to us; its authority for the Christian conscience is certainly different from that of reason. Thus for Christian ethics, its authority is inescapable without being absolute.

One is prone to inquire if the Bible can be set in a rank-order of authorities for Christian ethics. Where does it stand in the chain-of-command? Niebuhr suggests that this is the wrong question, and arises from false expectations. To use spatial language, authorities are related to each other horizontally as well as vertically: The church stands alongside of the Bible as an authority, but it also stands under the Bible. No simple diagram of authority in Christian morals can be drawn: there is an authority of the Spirit, of immediate intuitive assurance as is claimed most forcefully by the Quakers; there is an authority of reason which is associated with our nature, and which is related to the way in which we think ethically in the face of Scripture; nature itself has a mediate authority for Christian morality—there are certain demands made by our natural social existence dealt with in terms of natural law by some theologians, and orders of creation by others. Any effort to make a permanent and universal rank-order of these things *a priori* distorts and finally falsifies the reality of moral existence in the Christian community.

What can be said more positively about the authority of Scripture? An answer to this question falls along lines parallel to the uses that ethics as a critical discipline has for man's practical moral life. The Bible's authority is not infallible—it cannot tell inerrantly what the responsible man ought to say and do, but it is "truthfulness." The claim to moral infallibility falls into the quarrels of contradictory passages on moral questions. "They shall beat their swords into plowshares" (Isa. 2:4) and "You shall beat your plowshares into swords" (Joel 3:10). Not only are there the patent difficulties within Scripture, but it always stands in the presence of the interpreter who is fallible as well. But there is a truthfulness; the Bible is a dependable, reliable, honest, truthful witness to the life of men before God. Thus it can be a useful, but changing director of the thought and action of the Christian community.

One can therefore speak of its "educational authority." It is like the role of the teacher, which is to lead to a direct relationship of the student to the more ultimate authority of reality that the teacher mediates. It is important not because it gives us knowledge of itself, but because it gives us knowledge of God acting on men, and of ourselves before God; it gives us an understanding of the world in which we live; it gives us a meaningful and orderly view of life. Just as a scientist is under the authority of a method, a logic, and a discipline which identify him as a scientist, so the Christian community is under the influential authority of Scripture which brings its moral identity into being. The community cannot think the mind of Christ without the training of Scripture; it cannot know the God who calls it to responsibility apart from the study of Scripture. But Scripture always points to the authority which it mediates, and like the able teacher, seeks to make itself unnecessary.

Scripture can also be spoken of as a "corroborative authority." It is a court of validation for the judgments and actions of the Christian community and its members. The conscience is not determined exclusively and absolutely by the study of Scripture, but Christians bring matters of conscience to the Scripture and find in it a judgment or a corroboration. The Christian community is as capable of false rationalizations, of perverted and distorted purposes, as any other community. The Bible, as the court of validation, aids the Church in eliminating its perversities, and verifying its true purposes. In this usage, Scripture also has parallels to other human enterprises: for example, the legislation of the land is brought before the Constitution as a basis of validation through the interpretation of the Courts.

But the Bible does have an authority that is unique both in content and in function. It is for the Christian community the record of our faith as nowhere else found. It bears the authority of God's disclosure of himself. It tells the historical revelation of the transcendent One, the One who is outside our history, standing *over against* us. It is the story of Emmanuel—of God *with* us. It is also the story of the Spirit, of the immanent principle—the Holy Spirit's work in us. The Bible provides our theology, and there obviously cannot be Christian ethics without theology. It is in Scripture that we find the trinitarian pattern which is indispensable for understanding the ultimate authority for man's moral existence. God is disclosed as the Creator—the one in whom power is manifest, but goodness is uncertain. He is disclosed in the Son, as God with us— the one in whom goodness is present, but power is dubious. He is disclosed in the Holy Spirit—the one whose presence is manifest, but whose ultimate nature is shrouded in mystery. The Bible shows us in the Incarnation that power is goodness and goodness is power; our Christian faith and life are based upon the apprehending of this goodness and power of God. Thus Scripture is the unique and indispensable but mediate and derived authority for our knowledge of God and our existence before him.

The importance of the historical disclosure of God in the story of life and thought given in Scripture for Niebuhr might well miss the reader of the present book. It would have been the substance of a second volume of his ethics, that dealing with the "Principles of Christian Action." It would have elaborated the implications of statements in this book about response to God. Thus, with no possibility of this elaboration coming from the author himself, it is important to sketch out Niebuhr's interpretation of the God who discloses himself in all the actions upon us, the God to whose actions we respond in our actions.

RESPONSE TO GOD, WHO ACTS UPON US

"Responsibility affirms—God is acting in all actions upon you. So respond to all actions upon you as to respond to his action." (P. 126, below.) For most of H. Richard Niebuhr's students such a statement is the most memorable theme in his course of lectures on Christian ethics. It provides not only the most pregnant possibilities, but also some of the most difficult problems in his systematic thought. It combines the indicative and imperative in a subtle and significant way. And certainly it takes seriously the task of theological reflection for Christian ethics and for the moral life.

Sometimes Niebuhr was willing to say more, and sometimes less, about God who acts upon us. *Radical Monotheism* leaves some readers with the impression that God is best talked about in the abstract language of Being, in contrast to the more Biblical language that they find in *The Meaning of Revelation*. In part what he said at any one time was a response to his perception of distortions in the theological fads he found in students and Churchmen. The task of this introductory essay is not to describe shifts in emphasis in his thought, nor is it to claim a dominant and thoroughgoing consistency in his reflection. Rather, I shall attempt to delineate the main themes of his theology in relation to his ethics as these were developed over and over again in his systematic lecture course.

One can see what Niebuhr desires to affirm and to avoid in relation to some other theological ethics. He had deep appreciation for Luther's affirmation that God is the Actor, and that man is more acted upon than acting. But, as Chapter 5 of *Christ and Culture* indicates, there is too much duality in Luther's conception of God's relatedness to man and the world to permit Niebuhr to embrace Luther's view of "proper" and "alien" works of righteousness, of the "two realms," and of law and gospel. Niebuhr was religiously and theologically informed to the depths of his life and thought by affirmations of the divine sovereignty in the writings of Augustine, Calvin, and Jonathan Edwards.[9] Even the philosophical determinism of Spinoza enticed his sympathy and reflection at many points. But his statements of God's absoluteness and sovereignty were by no means footnotes on historical material. He could freely use the language of Being, but distinguished his own usage of it from that of Paul Tillich as well as of Thomas Aquinas—he confessed Edwards to be his intellectual mentor at this point. One might suspect that his penchant for *mono*theism and for a sovereign God might make him more congenial to the extensive theological program of Karl Barth with his singular

[9] The best analysis that we have of Niebuhr's theological background does not adequately develop the Augustinian, Reformation, Edwardsean, and generally American roots of Niebuhr's thought, as its author freely admits. See Hans Frei, "Niebuhr's Theological Background," in *Faith and Ethics*, pp. 9–64.

emphasis on Jesus Christ as the one in and through whom all things are created, ruled, and redeemed. But whereas the apparent duality between the Creative and the Redeeming work of God in Luther, and in Brunner's *Divine Imperative,* was excessive, the apparent collapse of important distinctions between the Creative, Sustaining, and Redeeming work of God into the inclusive exclusiveness of Christology in Barth was equally critically received. Niebuhr could say with F. D. Maurice that "the abyss of love is deeper than the abyss of death," and affirm with Maurice that grace is prior to sin in the order of things. But he did not bend such an assertion in a direction that made Barth's own similar affirmations a congenial theological home. Nor did he lose sight of God, the awesome Judge. The points of reference could be expanded at greater length than would be useful to the purpose of this essay. Niebuhr read most things first with a predisposition to be sympathetic toward an author; he was basically nonpolemical in his theological reflection. Thus even men against whom he delivered his most severe criticisms were often men from whom he learned most. But through and through, his reflections about God were impregnated by his Kantian mentality and his Troeltschian learning, which led him to take statements about God very seriously, without taking them with the seriousness that assumed he or any other man was making literal statements about the One beyond the Many.

To answer the question "Who is the God known to us in our action?" is in a sense to ask another question: "Who is the God known to the children of Israel, to Jesus Christ, to the early Church, and to the community in its history?" In the discussion of Niebuhr's view of Scripture in ethics, his basically trinitarian pattern of theology was indicated. God is our Creator—he manifests himself as power; God is our Governor and Judge—he manifests himself as order; God is our Redeemer—he manifests himself as goodness and mercy. Niebuhr's trinitarianism was not a defensive kind; that is, he was not interested in expounding a trinitarian ethic in order to prove his orthodoxy (a matter which gave him little concern). Nor does his derivation of a trinitarian pattern of God's disclosure to men in the Scripture lead to a kind of "therefore" thinking—God is Biblically disclosed in a trinitarian manner, therefore we postulate a doctrine of the Trinity from which we derive statements about how God is ruling us today. In his theological ethics the life of faith and the life of thought were more closely integrated than to permit any doctrinaire doctrinal thinking. God is not our Creator, Governor, and Redeemer *because* the Bible suggests this to us; rather what one finds in the life of the Biblical people is what one finds in the life of faith in the present. Both point to the reality that is objective to themselves. To understand God's revelation of himself to Biblical men is to understand God's disclosure of himself to us; to be aware of God's action upon us is also to be informed by God's action on Biblical events.

Thus for Niebuhr the importance of the trinitarian understanding of God is not to be understood in terms of the continuity of a pattern of ideas in the history of Christian thought. It is a part of the present experience of the moral community that understands itself as responsible to God, just as it has been part of the experience of the community since Biblical times. In his exposition of these things he did not communicate the impression that this theological side of ethics was a purely intellectual enterprise, raising objective metaphysical problems, and finding rational solutions to them. Niebuhr communicated to his students that in a deeply personal sense God was *his* Creator, God was *his* Sustainer and *his* Judge, God was *his* Redeemer. While this personal sense, this religious and moral consciousness, was present, God never became something private, or exclusively personal. He is the God of nature in all its vastness, the God of historical events in all their complexity, the God of death as well as of life.

It was not characteristic of Niebuhr's exposition to speak of God's relation to the world as if it had its own distinct historical chronology. Indeed, his view of revelation did not permit him to divide God's activity along some dispensational time line; as if first he created the world; then he governed and judged the world; then he redeemed it. He did create the world, to be sure; but the Creator is the Governor and the Redeemer, and always was so. And he continues to be creative in the world which he governs and redeems.[10] The action of the Sustainer and Judge is the action of the Creator and Redeemer. The action of God the Redeemer is the action of the Creator and Sustainer.

It is no more characteristic of Niebuhr to suggest that God is present now as Creator, then as Redeemer to the contemporary community, as if his presence was divisible into discrete moments when he would show one face and then the other. Rather he is present at the same time and in the same actions upon us as our Creator, Governor, and Redeemer. Here his dissatisfaction with Lutheran dogma is very apparent—for their right- and left-handed views of God, being the Creator and Governor with one hand, and the Redeemer with the other, violates Niebuhr's sense of God's Oneness, and his sense of the presence of redemption in the creative action of God, of ordering in the redemptive action of God, of God's graciousness in his judgment and his judgment in his grace. Further, for Niebuhr the redemptive work of God was not confined to his gracious remission of man's personal sin, and the restoration of a new personal relation to himself. The Redeemer is present in the ordering of the world through the establishment of justice, as well as in the forgiveness of each man's personal sin. He was so present to the sons of God in Israel, as he is also to his children in the Christian Church. He is acting as Creator,

---

[10] Niebuhr did not leave us with any precise exposition of Christology, and perhaps intentionally so. But many students might continue to wish for one in order to see how his theological themes might be related to each other through Christology, especially in our time of Christocentrism (excessively and deplorably so for Niebuhr).

Sustainer and Judge, and Redeemer in the events of the non-Christian (in a cultural sense) parts of the world as well as in the Christian West.

For purposes of theological-ethical analysis, however, we can make distinctions between our response to God the Creator, God the Governor, and God the Redeemer. We can analyze characteristics of response without judging the response itself to be segmented and clearly differentiated, in the same manner that we can affirm God to be Triune without denying that he is One. Thus Niebuhr developed major sections of his instruction in Christian ethics as "Response to God the Creator," "Response to God the Governor," and "Response to God the Redeemer." I shall briefly characterize typical presentations under these rubrics.

In Christian faith and life God is recognized as the Creator of all things. "Whatever is, is good" was axiomatic in Niebuhr's thought, and this led to an appreciative, affirmative disposition toward the world as his first response to it. From the Creation story in Genesis, from the testimony of the Psalms, and from Jesus' valuation of persons and things (for one must look at Jesus' life as well as his teachings), one can affirm that first, each thing is good in its particularity, and secondly, that all things are good in relationship to each other. What is testified to in Scripture is attested in life: even the sinner is good, and he can be good for others in some ways that a righteous man cannot be. It is attested in Augustine, in Christian poets, in St. Francis and John Woolman, in Calvin's affirmation that even the ruins of man ravaged by sin are noble. And the One who made all things good has made himself known in his creation and in his redeeming work as One who is loving. We are valued by God, just as the rest of creation is; thus we are free to love the goodness of the world without being preoccupied with our own value.

Our response of love to what God has created out of love can be analyzed in various stages. One can *merely accept* what is, which is only to affirm that the final judgment is not one's own. But beyond this one can also *affirm* oneself, the neighbor, and even the enemy. The world of nature is to be affirmed; indeed, in Christian eschatology one does not look for a passing of heaven and earth apart from the affirmation of a new heaven and a new earth. Affirmation of the world leads to the desire to *understand* it. One accepts, affirms, and then asks: "What is here?" "What is being said and done here?" Love of the good world, called forth by faith, leads in turn to a "scientific" response—to an understanding of the world of persons, the world of historical events, the world of nature. Further, one responds to the goodness of the action of God the Creator by the *cultivation* of the world that is in a state of becoming. The whole of human culture is the imposition of cultivating activity on a world unfashioned, or only in the process of being fashioned. The Christian responds by "tending" the world; man is not so much the creator of the world as he is its cultivator, its tender. And finally, man himself is created with the possibility of being *creative*. Man's response to God the Creator is to participate with his own limited creativity in the reality of God's creative action. He fashions things *like* the Creator fashions things; he makes things that were not there before—a symphony, a machine. At each of these stages, and particularly in the creative stage, the temptation to idolatry is present, which is in this context the temptation to forget that we are merely *responders,* that we are responding to God the Creator. But the reality of sin does not deny the possibility of an open, indeed, joyous response to the goodness being made possible by the action of God the Creator.

Man responds to God, the Sustainer and Judge, to God, the Sovereign Governor, which is in part to say that he responds to an ordered life. Ethics of Natural Law and ethics of the Orders of Creation particularly stress this aspect of moral existence, but each has its distorting tendencies, and each has its built-in difficulties. There is the problem of whether disordered man can discern the essential and right order of the world. There is a tendency to think statically rather than dynamically, to think of a once-for-all ordered creation rather than an ordering activity in creation. There is always the necessity to look at an order from a particular historical point of view, rather than from a value-free, unbound perspective. There is the tendency to distinguish too sharply between the ethics of creation and the ethics of redemption—a distinction common to Roman Catholicism, to Lutheranism, and to Emil Brunner's ethics. And finally the emphasis in ethics of law and order tends to be on universal patterns, rather than on the historical realities emerging under particular, individual conditions. But there is a propriety in the concern of such ethics that is not to be lost, namely, that man is engaged in ordering work within certain limits and possibilities, and that man must attend to the structures of human relationships that are in conformity to the divine government.

Moral action is human action in response to the governing action of God upon us. The most pervasive form in which God acts as our Governor is in the human experience of limitation, of finitude. Our finiteness is brought to our consciousness by our confrontation with other beings who limit us, or make us aware of our limits. (Niebuhr was persuaded that men do not encounter nonbeing per se, but rather meet their limits in relation to other beings.) Man is limited corporeally. He meets the limitations of his own physical capacity in an understanding of his dependence upon, for examples, a floor to support him, and air to breathe. He meets the limitations of his body in its temporal dimensions in the existence of his parents who were necessary for him to be, and in the forces that will bring him to his death. Man is mentally limited. Man's capacity to penetrate the thought of another person is limited not only by his own intellectual finiteness, but by the aspects of the experience of the other that one cannot make one's own. Our thought about the natural world also is limited by the reality of the objects about which we think. Man is limited in his selfhood: his action is limited by the capacities of his will; his emotions set limits to his rationality. Man is limited in his existence by the necessity of I-Thou relationships. The self depends upon dialogue with the other self for its own existence. The self confronts other selves who require acknowledgment and recognition.

A similar analysis can be made in the social sphere of human life. The historical possibilities of the American nation are limited by its own past history, by its natural resources, by its contemporary confrontation with other nations. We are limited by our cultural heritage, which defines in part what we are permitted to be and to do; we are limited by our own success in technology, which creates certain fears about our pace of self-destruction through weapons or through the misuses of nature; we are limited by the existence of the U.S.S.R. and other nations over against us.

God governs the world not only by the limits of others upon us, but also by using our bodies, our minds, our relationships, our national existence, to limit the existence of others. Just as a father is limited by his place of responsibility for his family, so the family is limited by the actions of the father. Just as our national allies limit us by their concerns to maintain their autonomy and identity, so we limit them by their dependence upon our support. Just as our actions are limited by the U.S.S.R., so the actions of the U.S.S.R. are limited by our power.

Niebuhr was not inclined to interpret the limitations of the governing action of God in terms of its negative qualities alone, in terms of what might be perceived to be threats coming from finiteness. The web of limitations is a web of sustaining support. God is Governor both in the sense of the one who rules us with objective power through the other being, and the Sustainer who preserves and enhances our existence through others. Not only does one experience pain and suffering through the limitations of other beings upon him; he also experiences joy and affirmation through them. Not only does one cause pain and sufferings to the others by being the limiter of their existence; he sustains them and brings to them joy and goodness.

The situation of limitation is universal. It can be responded to in unbelief or in faith. In unbelief it may lead to a struggle in which men say "not thy will, but *mine* be done," into the division of the world into two exclusive camps—our own and our enemies', our goodness and the evil of the other. This one observes, for example, in the view of international relations that does not see how God can be governing us by the existence of an equally strong power, and that this is to our good as well as to the other nation's. Or in unbelief, one might assume that the heart of the moral problem is exclusively in the self—in its will alone. The morally sensitive unbeliever is often tempted to misconstrue the moral order by believing that the enemy of goodness is not complex in human relatedness, but existent in individual incapacity, or in the power of desire. Such sensitive souls as Spinoza and Tolstoy seemed to bend in this direction.

But one can respond to the situation of limitation in faith. The radical monotheistic faith that Niebuhr espoused was faith in God who sovereignly rules over all, so that no power that is on earth is there except by the power of God. In the Biblical accounts we find that the Assyrians and Pilate were not identified as totally evil powers, but each was there within the sovereign purposes and actions of God. There are, of course, eschatological dimensions to the rule of God; we look forward to his Kingdom. But the Bible witnesses to his present power and authority. For ethics this means that one interprets the powers that limit and sustain him as powers in the service of God's governing action. One responds to the rise of Marxism first of all in repentance, seeing how it judges the injustices and the class-interests of "Christian" communities. One sees in it God's judgment and limitation of our own nation and culture, and responds to it in actions that are corrective of the abuses out of which it emerged. One responds to personal suffering first in terms of repentance, seeing how it has often been brought on by one's own misdeeds and self-will.

To explicate this view, Niebuhr was partial to the political or social analogy. In dealing with it, it is clear that he is not interested in an intellectual system which will objectively tidy up the problems of theodicy as if these were purely rational, logical problems. He is here, as at all points, analyzing the living response of living men of faith. God is the king; he is the lawgiver and the judge. He is also the sustainer and rewarder of life: "Honor thy father and thy mother *that* thy days may be long . . ." He rules in such fashion that the Deuteronomic pattern cannot be ignored in favor of some futuristic eschatology: the dust storms on the American prairies are signs of man's sinful exploitation of the soil in his failure to respond properly to God's governing action. "Whom the Lord loveth he chastiseth"—pain and suffering are opportunities for growth of the human spirit. Men do suffer vicariously for the deeds of others; the consequences of human deeds and errors spread through the related parts of the human community. And we are often responsible for the misdeeds of others; this is the truth in the social theories of delinquent behavior. God, the Sovereign Ruler, governs, sustains, and judges us through his actions in history, in interpersonal experiences, and in nature.

In this light, then, the Christian community views its place in the limitations. Often Niebuhr developed the Christian community's response under the rubric of self-denial, but not in a traditional monastic sense. The latter he viewed as an effort to escape from situations of limitation that require a more demanding existential responsibility and self-denial. Celibacy may be an escape from the limitations of existence in the family; poverty an escape from the responsibilities of property; humility may better occur in being humiliated by others in the web of social relations than in the cloister. Self-denial for Niebuhr was not self-detachment or self-hatred (he often criticized Erich Fromm's interpretation of Christianity in this and other regards); it is rather quiet acceptance, repentance, and cross-bearing in relation to the governing action of God through the beings that limit us. It is the acceptance of God's acceptance of human limitations. It is the affirmation in relationships of the divine will, rather than the will of any finite agents of God's will. Self-denial is always relevant to the actual situation in which we find ourselves—as member of a family, as professor or pastor or factory worker, as citizen in our nation and its time in history. It is the acceptance of a restricted field of operation, of having to act within the limits of our sphere. It is the affirmation of the value of others. It is a life of preliminary judgments, struggles, and victories in the hope of the last judgment and the resurrection. It moves toward creative, sustaining, and liberating action in service to others. It is acceptance of our responsibility to limit others, even in the knowledge of the fact that our action is never fully right, that our action causes suffering to others (as in war). It is the acknowledgment that our restraining activity (for examples, in family or in nation) is under the restraint of others, and thus is not to be enacted only with self-restraint but with acceptance of the restraint of others upon it.[11]

The Divine Ruler, our Sustainer and Judge, is also our Redeemer. Thus the Christian life is a response to the redeeming action of God. The creative, governing, and redeeming actions of God are not easily separable; nor are the events in which we respond to them discretely creative in one instance, ruling in another, and redemptive in a third, as we have indicated. This is important to recall in thinking about our response to God's redeeming work, for Christians are often tempted to assert that the uniqueness of Christian ethics is that they are "redemptive ethics," or that the

[11] In this context Niebuhr always discussed the issue of Christian pacifism, and made his case of "conscientious participation" in war, the call to be the restrainer, as well as to be restrained.

moral uniqueness of the Church is that it is a redeeming community. These assertions are errors, according to Niebuhr, as shall be shown.

Indeed, for Niebuhr God's redemptive action could not be isolated and confined to a single act. God the Redeemer is the Eternal Son, the Eternal Christ, "pre-existent and post-existent"; thus no single act of his is to be absolutized as the redemptive act. If God is Redeemer, he is always Redeemer, he was always Redeemer, he will always be Redeemer. But certain acts are revelatory of the redemptive action of God in all of history.[12] The Exodus is a revelation of God the Redeemer; for Christians and for all mankind the act of God in Christ is revelatory of God the Redeemer. God's revelatory act itself is redemptive: the Exodus changed the history of the children of Israel; and through God's act in Jesus Christ the history of the world has been changed.

Attempts to fix redemption on acts of the past, or wholly on a future act, are both distorted. God is the Redeemer in all his acts. The past acts of redemption are not real unless they are re-enacted in the present life; the future acts of redemption are not meaningful unless pre-enacted in the present.

Various polarities (a favorite pattern of thought for Niebuhr) can be used to explicate the meaning of God's redeeming work. One is the objective-subjective polarity: Jesus Christ is Lord, the power of sin is broken, though all may not yet recognize it, to use some of the language of F. D. Maurice. This is the objective pole. But until this has become revelatory truth for persons, nothing has happened. Thus one has the subjective side as well. Christ is the believer's in faith, as well as the Universal Lord; both poles are true. Another is the "theoretical-voluntary" polarity. One can understand that the redemptive power is real, and present; but apart from the act of will, the act of belief, nothing occurs. Another is

[12] Here, as elsewhere, the reader may wish to turn to *The Meaning of Revelation* for a more extensive explication.

the polarity of person and community. Redemption has a personal character: *my* guilt is forgiven. Yet redemption has a communal character: the whole world is redeemed. And there is present the polarity of the divine-human dialogue: God acts redemptively, but there is no redemption until free men respond to the divine act. Man responds to God in the exercise of his will, his created freedom; thus God can give man through his redemption a new freedom.

What can be said about the ethics of redemption that are evoked by God the Redeemer? In the first instance we can begin to define what they are not. Ethics of redemption are *not* redemptive ethics, ethics that seek to redeem. Ethics that seek to redeem rest on a fundamental error of confusing the action of God with the action of men. It is not the action of the church that redeems a member of the community; it is God's action that is redemptive. It is not the converted man who redeems his neighbor through an act of love; it is God who redeems him. The notion that the Christian community is a redemptive community fails to make this basic distinction between the divine and the human, and this leads to aspirations to perfectionism in its life and to pride.

The ethics of redemption are *not* the ethics of the redeemed. They are not the private property of a particular group in history and cannot be equated with any group that claims to be the "redeemed." Indeed, the redeemed are those who are free from the burdens of the past, free from having to claim ethics of their own, free to be creative. And the ethics of redemption are *not* to be associated with the religion of redemption in the fashion of the Ritschlians. The religion of redemption has been related to ethics in two ways: first, as giving the inner motivation and impulse to be ethical, and second, as providing forgiveness for men in their ethical failure. If this duality is carried out, however, we often begin to confine the divine action to the realm of religion and the church, and human action to the realm of civil life. Against such divisions, Niebuhr affirmed that the redemptive work of God is beyond and in the work of man in the sphere of religion *and* in the sphere of ethics in the church and in the world.

From what does God redeem us, and to what are we redeemed? As the New Testament claims, we are redeemed from sin, from the law, evil, and from death. We are redeemed from centering life upon the self, and from our immaturity. We are redeemed from a life of negation to a life of pure grace. The life of grace to which we are redeemed is a life of freedom, a life free of defensiveness. It is a life of love (more in terms of Augustine's exposition in *The Morals of the Catholic Church* than in terms of Nygren's exposition of *agape* in *Agape and Eros*). We are free to relate ourselves to the good that is present in perverted forms; we are free to love that which is good, attractive, and worthy in relation to God. We are redeemed to a life of service. Luther's brief treatise "On the Liberty of the Christian Man" was a favorite of Niebuhr's in expounding the theme of service. We are loved, we are justified by God's redeeming action; therefore, we can live and we can serve the neighbor in love. God redeems us from the need for self-justification, and frees us to serve the need and the will of the neighbor. We are redeemed to eternal life—to a new life in the Spirit as the Gospel of John and as St. Paul's letters expound this. We have the assurance that God gives us new life in the Spirit, eternal life in our existence.

We can analyze the characteristics of the Christian life as life in response to redemption in a way that we cannot set forth statements about the Christian ethics of redemption. It is the life in which one freely gives because he freely receives. It is a life of joy. It is a life of forgiveness, and gratitude, a life that changes our relationships to others. It has all these indicative elements, and has as well its own imperatives. It is a life of liberty that is not given to the excesses of the flesh, to boasting, and to the exclusion of others from the circle of love. We are not to fall back into new yokes of bondage. We are to forgive others as we have been forgiven, to serve others as we have been served.

The effect of God's redeeming action is not, in the end, the creation of "ethics of redemption." Its effect is *to qualify all the existing relations* that we have; it is a transformation and transvaluation of all our actions. It leads us, for example, to attack the evil in ourselves as we attack the external evils around us; it moves us in all our relations to others to seek their good, to seek and to save the lost; it impregnates our actions with freedom and love so that we are driven toward the creative responses to others that realize the good.

In Niebuhr's exposition of the life of response to the actions of God upon us through the actions of others, we have important elements of his systematic thought that are given in the present book only in an attenuated form, or sometimes only pointed to. The Robertson Lectures develop the pattern of the life of response, the life of responsibility. Thus it reveals to us the mind of the philosopher of the Christian life. In the Appendix to this book we begin to see Niebuhr, the theologian of the Christian life, in the fullness that this was present in his teaching. Theology, he often said, is reflection on the action and nature of God; ethics is reflection on the response of man to the action and nature of God. One can see from this definition of Christian ethics that the philosopher of the Christian life had to be its theologian in order to develop a systematic Christian ethics, for the moral life of the Christian community *is response to God,* the Creator, the Governor, and the Redeemer. If this introductory essay aids the reader in recalling or seeing for the first time how the responsible self is related to the action of God, the Father, the Son, and the Holy Spirit, God the Father of our Lord Jesus Christ, it has achieved its limited purpose. No one is more aware than its author of its deficiencies, and no one wishes more than he that H. Richard Niebuhr could have written for himself a volume on "The Principles of Christian Action," and a third on "Christian Responsibility in the Common Life."

Prologue: On Christian Moral Philosophy

THE FOLLOWING Robertson Lectures on *The Responsible Self* have been given the subtitle "An Essay in Christian Moral Philosophy" in order that a prospective reader may have some forewarning about what to expect. My approach to the subject is neither theological nor philosophical in the sense in which these terms are employed for the most part by professional workers in both groups. Since neither recognizes the logical or academic legitimacy of a "Christian moral philosophy," neither will be led to expect anything here of which he might want to take account. I use the term, philosophy, in the quite nontechnical though widely accepted meaning of love of wisdom or understanding and want to say by my subtitle simply that these are the reflections of a Christian who is seeking to understand the mode of his existence and that of his fellow beings as human agents.

The point of view is that of a Christian believer; the object to be understood is man's moral life; the method is philosophical in this broad sense defined. Something further may need to be said on each of these counts.

I call myself a Christian though there are those who challenge my right to that name, either because they require a Christian to maintain some one of various sets of beliefs that I do not hold or because they require him to live up to some one of various sets of moral standards, including those of my own conscience, to which I do not conform. I call myself a Christian simply because I also am a follower of Jesus Christ, though I travel at a great distance from him not only in time but in the spirit of my traveling; because I believe that my way of thinking about life, myself, my human companions and our destiny has been so modified by his presence in our history that I cannot get away from his influence; and also because I do not want to get away from it; above all, I call myself a Christian because my relation to God has been, so far as I can see, deeply conditioned by this presence of Jesus Christ in my history and in our history. In one sense I must call myself a Christian in the same way that I call myself a twentieth-century man. To be a Christian is simply part of my fate, as it is the fate of another to be a Muslim or a Jew. In this sense a very large part of mankind is today Christian; it has come under the influence of Jesus Christ so that even its Judaism and Mohammedanism bears witness to the fact that Jesus Christ has been among us. But I call myself a Christian more because I have both accepted this fateful fact and because I identify myself with what I understand to be the cause of Jesus Christ. That cause I designate simply as the reconciliation of man to God. The term doubtless needs much explanation. It is used in many contexts and can carry with it overtones of guilt feelings, of ideas of blood atonement, etc., etc. I will quarrel with no one about the precise ways in which Jesus Christ reconciles men to God or challenges men to undertake with him the ministry of reconciliation. I am quite certain that reconciliation, as the establishment of friendship between God and man—between the power by which all things are and this human race of ours—has more aspects to it than have been dreamed of in our theologies. Jesus Christ is for me, as for many of my fellow Christians, the one who lived and died and rose again for this cause of bringing God to men and men to God and so also of reconciling men to each other and to their world. The establishment of this friendship is to me the key problem in human existence. Because through Jesus Christ—his fate—as well as by him—that is, his ministry—this has become evident to me; because in him I see the prospect of my own reconciliation; because I have been challenged to make this cause my own—therefore I call myself a Christian.

The word, Christian, therefore, defines my point of view and my perspective. I have debated with myself whether the term to be employed to define the standpoint is not theistic rather than Christian. A theistic moral philosophy I conceive as one which takes as its starting point man's existence as lived in relation to God, as a naturalistic moral philosophy begins with man as living in and from nature. Or it is one which posits that in all man's seeking he seeks God, as a hedonistic philosophy begins with desire for pleasure as the datum in man's life. The point of view here is theistic. I am not arguing from nature to God nor from morality to God; though to some readers some parts of this book may seem to have the character of moral arguments for God's existence, the conduct of such an argument has not been part of my intention. I believe that man exists and moves and has his being in God; that his fundamental relation is to God. That is the starting point, not the conclusion: hence the temptation to call this a theistic moral philosophy. But though God's relation to man is not qualified by man's acceptance or rejection of his presence, man's relation to God is evidently so qualified. I cannot think about God's relation to man in the abstract. The historical qualification of my relation to him is inescapable. I cannot presume to think as a Jew or a Mohammedan would think about God, though I recognize that they are thinking about the same God about whom I think. Nor can I presume to rise above those specific relations to God in which I have been placed so as to think simply and theistically about God. There is no such being, or source of being, surely, as a Christian God (though there may be Christian idols); but there is a Christian relation to God and I cannot abstract from that, as no Jew or Mohammedan can abstract from a Jewish or Muslim relation. So much must be said for the point of view, which I do not undertake to defend as a philosophic point of view, though so far as I can see every philosopher also has a standpoint, which he often fails to confess.

The object of the inquiry is not, as in the case of Christian ethics, simply the Christian life but rather human moral life in general. It is at this point that I part company with many theologians who tend to deal with the Christian life as though it were somehow discontinuous with other modes of human existence. To be sure, the Christian life has its own style; there is such a thing as a Christian ethics which can be distinguished from a naturalistic or a hedonistic ethics, and I do not challenge the need for Christian ethics as the critical examination of that life. Indeed I move toward a Christian ethics in the later chapters of this essay in Christian moral philosophy. But my concern here is with the understanding of our human life from a Christian point of view and neither with the understanding of Christian life from some other point of view (such as that of social adjustment or adaptation to nature) nor with the understanding of Christian life only, from a Christian point of view.

Finally, the term, philosophy, requires some further justification. I regard this effort as an essay in Christian moral *philosophy* for two reasons. First, because I am concerned in it in part with the development of an instrument of analysis which applies to any form of human life including the Christian. All life has the character of responsiveness, I maintain. We interpret the actions to which we respond differently, to be sure, but we do respond, whether we interpret them as actions of God or of the devil or of a blindly running atom. Secondly, it is more philosophy than theology in the current understanding of theology, because my approach is not Bible-centered, though I think it is Bible-informed. If I dissent from those philosophers who undertake to analyze the moral life as though that life were nonhistorical, as though the ideas and words of the English moral language referred to the pure emotions of nonhistorical beings or to pure concepts, I find myself equally ill at ease with theologians who deal with the Scriptures as a nonhistorical book and undertake to explain it as though they were nonhistorical men.

H. R. N.

1

THE MEANING OF RESPONSIBILITY

THE WORD *responsibility* and cognate terms are widely used in our time when men speak about that phase of human existence to which they customarily referred in the past with the aid of such signs as *moral* and *good*. The *responsible citizen,* the *responsible society,* the *responsibilities of our office* and similar phrases are often on our lips. This meaning of *responsibility* is of relatively recent origin. There was a time when *responsible* meant *correspondent* as in the statement "The mouth large but not responsible to so large a body." But its use in sentences such as "The great God has treated us as responsible beings," seems to have become common only in the nineteenth and twentieth centuries.[1] It is a relatively late-born child, therefore, in the family of words in which duty, law, virtue, goodness, and morality are its much older

---

[1] *Oxford English Dictionary.*

siblings. This history may mean nothing more, of course, than that men have found a new sign for a well-known phenomenon and an old idea; many writers, indeed, so use it, as their definitions plainly show. But it is also possible that the word gives us a new symbol with which to grasp and understand not a really well-known phenomenon or an old idea but the actuality of that human existence of which other aspects came into view when we employed the older symbols of *the mores,* or of *the ethos,* or of *what is due,* or of *being virtuous,* that is, being manly. I believe that this is the case; the symbol of responsibility contains, as it were, hidden references, allusions, and similes which are in the depths of our mind as we grope for understanding of ourselves and toward definition of ourselves in action. But we are not concerned with the word nor with our subjective intentions as we use it. Our task rather is to try with the aid of this symbol to further the double purpose of ethics: to obey the ancient and perennial commandment, *"Gnothi seauton,"* "Know thyself"; and to seek guidance for our activity as we decide, choose, commit ourselves, and otherwise bear the burden of our necessary human freedom.

In the history of man's long quest after knowledge of himself as agent—that is, as a being in charge of his conduct—he has used fruitfully several other symbols and concepts in apprehending the form of his practical life and in giving shape to it in action. The most common symbol has been that of the maker, the fashioner. What is man like in all his actions? The suggestion readily comes to him that he is like an artificer who constructs things according to an idea and for the sake of an end. Can we not apply to the active life as a whole the image we take from our technical working in which we construct wheels and arrows, clothes and houses and ships and books and societies? So not only common-sense thinking about ideals, and ends and means, but much sophisticated philosophy has construed human existence. Thus Aristotle begins his *Ethics*—the most influential book in the West in this field—

with the statement: "Every art and every inquiry and similarly every action and pursuit, is thought to aim at some good."[2] Beyond all the arts of bridle-making and horse-riding and military strategy there must be then, he says, an art of arts, a master art, whose end is the actualization of the good man and the good society, whose material is human life itself. For the Greek philosopher and many who knowingly or unknowingly follow him, man is the being who makes himself—though he does not do so by himself—for the sake of a desired end. Two things in particular we say about ourselves: we act toward an end or are purposive; and, we act upon ourselves, we fashion ourselves, we give ourselves a form. Aristotle's great Christian disciple saw eye to eye with him. "Of the actions done by man," wrote Thomas Aquinas, "those alone are called properly *human,* which are proper to man as man. Now man differs from the irrational creatures in this, that he is master of his own acts. . . . But man is master of his own acts by reason and will: hence free-will is said to be *a function of will and reason.* Those actions, therefore, are properly called *human,* which proceed from a deliberate will. . . . Now it is clear that all the actions that proceed from any power are caused by that power acting in reference to its object. But the object of the will is some end in the shape of good. Therefore all human actions must be for an end."[3]

The image of man-the-maker who, acting for an end, gives shape to things is, of course, refined and criticized in the course of its long use, by idealists and utilitarians, hedonists and self-realizationists. But it remains a dominant image. And it has a wide range of applicability in life. Purposiveness and humanity do seem to go

[2] *The Works of Aristotle,* ed. W. D. Ross (Oxford: Clarendon Press, 1925), Vol. IX, *Ethica Nicomachea,* Bk. I, 1.

[3] *Summa Theologica,* Prima Secundae, Q. I., Resp. Translation above by J. Rickaby, S.J., *Aquinas Ethicus* (London: Burns and Oates, Ltd., 1896), Vol. I.

together. Everyone, even a determinist undertaking to demonstrate the truth of determinism, knows what it is to act with a purpose or a desired future state of affairs in mind, and knows also how important it is to inquire into the fitness of the steps taken moment by moment in his movement toward the desired goal. In most affairs of life we employ this practical ends-and-means reasoning and ask about our purposes. Education has its goals and so has religion; science is purposive though it defines its purpose only as knowledge of fact or as truth. Justice uses the idea when it asks about the culpability of the accused by raising the further question concerning his intentions and his ability to foresee consequences. Legislation thinks teleologically, that is, with respect to the telos—the goal—when it inquires into the desires of individual citizens and the various social groups, taking for granted that they all pursue some ends, whether these be power or prosperity or peace or pleasure; and when it raises the further question how manifold individual purposes can be organized into one common social purpose. Moral theories and moral exhortations to a large extent presuppose the future-directed, purposive character of human action and differ for the most part only—though seriously enough—in the ends they recommend or accept as given with human nature itself. The will to pleasure, the will to live, the will to power, the will to self-fulfillment, the will to love and be loved, the will to death and many another hormetic drive may be posited as most natural to man, whether as most compulsive or as setting before him the most attractive future state of affairs. When we are dealing with this human nature of ours, in ourselves and in others, as administrators of our private realms of body and mind or as directors of social enterprises—from families seeking happiness to international societies seeking peace—we cannot fail to ask: "At what long- or short-range state of affairs are we aiming, and what are the immediate steps that must be taken toward the attainment of the possible goal?" So the teleologist, in that double process of self-definition we call morals, interprets human life and seeks to direct it. The symbol of man-the-maker of many things and of himself also throws light not only on many enterprises but also on this strange affair of personal existence itself. The freedom of man appears in this context as the necessity of self-determination by final causes; his practical reason appears as his ability to distinguish between inclusive and exclusive, immediate and ultimate ends and to relate means to ends.

The men who have employed this image of man-the-maker in understanding and in shaping their conduct have, of course, by no means been unanimous in their choice of the ideals to be realized nor in their estimate of the potentialities of the material that is to be given the desired or desirable form. Whether the human end is to be achieved for the sake of delight or for further use toward another end, whether it is to be designed for the delight or the use of the self, or of the immediate society or of a universal community—these remain questions endlessly debated and endlessly submitted to individuals for personal decision. But the debates and decisions are carried on against the background of a common understanding of the nature of our personal existence. We are in all our working on selves—our own selves or our companions—technicians, artisans, craftsmen, artists.

Among many men and at many times another grand image of the general character of our life as agents prevails. It is the image of man-the-citizen, living under law. Those who conceive themselves and human beings in general with the aid of this great symbol point out the inadequacies and defects, as they see them, of that view of personal life which interprets it as *technē* or as art. In craftsmanship, they say, both the end and the means are relatively under our control. But neither is at our disposal when we deal with ourselves as persons or as communities.

Man-the-maker can reject material which does not fit his purposes. It is not so when the material is ourselves in our individual

and in our social nature. Our body, our sensations, our impulses—
these have been given us; whether to have them or not have them
is not under our control. We are with respect to these things not
as the artist is to his material but as the ruler of a city is to its
citizens. He must take them for better or for worse. And so it is
also with respect to the future. The favors or disfavors of fortune, as well as the "niggardly provisions of a step-motherly nature," put us at the mercy of alien powers so far as the completion
of our lives as works of art is concerned. What use would it have
been, had Socrates designed for himself that happy life which
Aristotle described? This life we live amidst our fellow men and
in the presence of nature's forces cannot be built over many generations like a cathedral. Who can plan his end? Who can by taking
thought guarantee that his being, his character, his work, will endure even in the memory of those that come after? Neither the
material then with which we work nor the future building is under
our control when the work is directed toward ourselves. This life
of ours is like politics more than it is like art, and politics is the
art of the possible. What is possible to us in the situation in which
we find ourselves? That we should rule ourselves as being ruled,
and not much more.

Many moral philosophers and theologians, otherwise disagreeing
with each other, agree at least in this, that they understand the
reality of our personal existence with the aid of the political image.
It is indeed, as in the case of the technical symbol, more than an
image for it is derived from our actual living. As a symbol it represents the use of a *special* experience for the interpretation of *all*
experience, of a part for the whole. We come to self-awareness if
not to self-existence in the midst of *mores,* of commandments and
rules, *Thou shalt*s and *Thou shalt not*s, of directions and permissions. Whether we begin with primitive man with his sense of
themis, the law of the community projected outward into the total
environment, or with the modern child with father and mother

images, with repressions and permissions, this life of ours, we say, must take account of morality, of the rule of the mores, of the ethos, of the laws and the law, of heteronomy and autonomy, of self-directedness and other-directedness, of approvals and disapprovals, of social, legal, and religious sanctions. This is what our total life is like, and hence arise the questions we must answer: "To what law shall I consent, against what law rebel? By what law or system of laws shall I govern myself and others? How shall I administer the domain of which I am the ruler or in which I participate in rule?"

As in the case of the symbol of the maker, the symbol of the citizen has a wide range of applicability in common life and has been found useful by many a special theorist. In intellectual action, for instance, man not only directs his thoughts and investigations toward the realization of a system of true knowledge that will be useful to other ends or give delight in itself, but carries on his work of observation, conceptualization, comparison, and relation under laws of logic or of scientific method. It is important for him, if he is a person and not only a reasoning animal, that he govern his inquiries by adherence to such rules or laws. Again, what man does in the political realm is not only or perhaps even primarily to seek the ends of order, peace, prosperity, and welfare but to do all that he does under the rule of justice. If we are to associate the two symbols with each other, as indeed we often do, we must say that justice itself is an end, though when we do this peculiar difficulties arise. The image has applicability to all our existence in society. We come into being under the rules of family, neighborhood, and nation, subject to the regulation of our action by others. Against these rules we can and do rebel, yet find it necessary—morally necessary, that is—to consent to some laws and to give ourselves rules, or to administer our lives in accordance with some discipline.

Again, as in the case of the maker image, those who employ

the citizen symbol for the understanding and regulation of self-conduct, have various domains in view. For some the republic that is to be governed is mostly that of the multifarious self, a being which is a multiplicity seeking unity or a unity diversifying itself into many roles. It is a congeries of many hungers and urges, of fears and angers and loves that is contained somehow within one body and one mind, which are two, yet united. The multiplicity of the body is matched by an at least equal variety of mental content. How to achieve that unity of the self, that organization of manifoldness we call personality, is a challenging question for the administrative self. It is not done in fact without external rule and regulation, but also not without internal consent and self-legislation. How this self-government is in fact achieved is one of the problems of much psychology and the concern of moralists. Or the republic in view is a human community of selves in which the manifoldness is that of many persons with many desires and subject to many regulations issuing from each other. The communal life then is considered as both consenting to law and as law-giving. Or again, the community we have in mind may be universal society, and the quest may be after those laws of nature or that will of the universal God which the person is asked to accept not only with consent but actively, as legislating citizen in a universal domain.

The effort so to conceive the self in its agency as legislative, obedient, and administrative has had a long history. Its use has raised many theoretical and practical problems, but it has also been very fruitful. The symbol of man the law-maker and law-abider may be a primordial or only a cultural symbol; but in any case it has been helpful in enabling us to understand large areas of our existence and to find guidance in the making of complex decisions.

II

IN THE history of theoretical ethics, but also in practical decisions, the use of these two great symbols for the understanding of our personal existence as self-acting beings has led to many disputes as well as to many efforts at compromise and adjustment. Those who consistently think of man-as-maker subordinate the giving of laws to the work of construction. For them the right is to be defined by reference to the good; rules are utilitarian in character; they are means to ends. All laws must justify themselves by the contribution they make to the attainment of a desired or desirable end. Those, however, who think of man's existence primarily with the aid of the citizen image seek equally to subordinate the good to the right; only right life is good and right life is no future ideal but always a present demand. Federalist schools, as they have been called by C. D. Broad, tend to say that we cannot apprehend our existence with the aid of one image but must employ both. They leave us as a rule with a double theory, of which the two parts remain essentially unharmonized. The conflict of theories is but an extension of the practical one which takes place in the personal and social life as we try to answer the questions: "What shall *I* do?" or "What shall *we* do?" We find ourselves moving there from the debate about the various ideals according to which we might shape our personal and social existence to the debate about what is required or demanded and by whom it is required. Or the movement may be from debate about the law to be obeyed to the question: "What laws can be justified in view of the ideal before us?" Practical debate on the achievement of desegregation, for example, moves between the insistence that the law of the country must be obeyed and the young Negroes' demand that the ideal state of affairs be realized.

What these debates suggest to us is that helpful as the fundamental images are which we employ in understanding and directing ourselves they remain images and hypotheses, not truthful copies of reality, and that something of the real lies beyond the borders of the image; something more and something different needs to be thought and done in our quest for the truth about ourselves and in our quest for true existence.

In this situation the rise of the new symbolism of responsibility is important. It represents an alternative or an additional way of conceiving and defining this existence of ours that is the material of our own actions. What is implicit in the idea of responsibility is the image of man-the-answerer, man engaged in dialogue, man acting in response to action upon him. As in the case of maker and of citizen, man-the-answerer offers us a synecdochic analogy. In trying to understand ourselves in our wholeness we use the image of a part of our activity; only now we think of all our actions as having the pattern of what we do when we answer another who addresses us. To be engaged in dialogue, to answer questions addressed to us, to defend ourselves against attacks, to reply to injunctions, to meet challenges—this is common experience. And now we try to think of all our actions as having this character of being responses, answers, to actions upon us. The faculty psychology of the past which saw in the self three or more facient powers, and the associationist psychology which understood the mind to operate under laws of association, have been replaced by a psychology of interaction which has made familiar to us the idea that we act in reaction to stimuli. Biology and sociology as well as psychology have taught us to regard ourselves as beings in the midst of a field of natural and social forces, acted upon and reacting, attracted and repelling. We try also to understand history less by asking about the ideals toward which societies and their leaders directed their efforts or about the laws they were obeying and more by inquiring into the challenges in their natural and social environment to which the societies were responding. It will not do to say that the older images of the maker and the citizen have lost their meaning in these biological, psychological, sociological, and historical analyses, but when we compare a modern psychology, a modern study of society, a modern history, with older examples of similar studies the difference thrusts itself upon one. The pattern of thought now is interactional, however much other great images must continue to be used to describe how we perceive and conceive, form associations, and carry on political, economic, educational, religious, and other enterprises.

The use of this image in the field of ethics is not yet considerable. When the word, responsibility, is used of the self as agent, as doer, it is usually translated with the aid of the older images as meaning direction toward goals or as ability to be moved by respect for law.[4] Yet the understanding of ourselves as responsive beings, who in all our actions answer to action upon us in accordance with our interpretation of such action, is a fruitful conception, which brings into view aspects of our self-defining conduct that are obscured when the older images are exclusively employed.

The understanding of ourselves with the aid of this image has been prefigured, as it were, by certain observations made by moralists of an older time. Aristotle may have had something of the sort in mind (something of the idea of what we would call a fitting response) when he described what he meant by the *mean* which constitutes virtue. He said that to feel fear, confidence, appetite, anger, and pity "at the right times, with reference to the right objects, towards the right people, with the right motive and in the right way, is what is intermediate and best. . . ."[5] Stoic ethics is

---

[4] Cf. W. Fales, *Wisdom and Responsibility* (Princeton: Princeton University Press, 1946). "There is much evidence that man is . . . determined by final ends which are not an object of his contemplation although they account for his personality and constitute his will. The pressure which the final ends exert upon man is felt as responsibility" (pp. 4 f.). Fales tries to account for the *feeling* of responsibility but never analyzes that feeling itself. Cf. pp. 56–58, 67, 71, 144.

[5] *Op. cit.,* Bk. II, 6.

usually interpreted as either primarily teleological or as primarily concerned with law; but it receives much of its peculiar character from the way in which it deals with the ethics of suffering, that is, with the responses which are to be made to the actions upon them that men must endure. The Stoic's main question is: "How may one react to events not with passion—that is, as one who is passive or who is subject to raw emotions called forth by events—but with reason?" And this reason for him is not first of all the law-giving power which rules the emotions, nor yet the purposive movement of the mind seeking to realize ideals. It is rather the interpretative power which understands the rationale in the action to which the self is subject and so enables it to respond rationally and freely rather than under the sway of passion. In Spinoza this idea of response guided by rational interpretation of the events and beings to which the self reacts plays a major role. To be sure, he is an idealist after a fashion, who asks how he may "discover and acquire the faculty of enjoying throughout eternity continual supreme happiness."[6] But he quickly notes that this end is not attainable except through that correction of the understanding which will permit men to substitute for the unclear and self-centered, emotion-arousing interpretations of what happens to them, a clear, distinct interpretation of all events as intelligible, rational events in the determined whole. The freedom of man from his passions, and from the tyranny of events over him exercised via the passions, is freedom gained through correct interpretation with the consequent changing of responses by the self to the events that go on within it and happen to it. Other intimations of the idea of response are to be found in naturalistic ethics and Marxism.

Outside the realm of philosophic theory practical life has made

---

[6] *Tractatus de intellectus emendatione*, I, 1. (The English translations of this treatise that I have consulted do not carry over the paragraph divisions by numerals that stand in the Latin text. However, the sentence quoted above occurs at the virtual beginning of the essay.—Ed.)

this approach to the solution of the problem of our action almost inevitable in two particular situations, in social emergencies and in personal suffering. It has often been remarked that the great decisions which give a society its specific character are functions of emergency situations in which a community has had to meet a challenge. Doubtless ideals, hopes and drives toward a desirable future play their part in such decisions; inherited laws are also important in them. Yet the decision on which the future depends and whence the new law issues is a decision made in response to action upon the society, and this action is guided by interpretation of what is going on. The emergence of modern America out of the Civil War when measures were adopted in response to challenges that the founding fathers had not foreseen; the welfare-state decisions of the New Deal era in reaction to depression and the entrance of the nation into the sphere of international politics in reaction to foreign wars despite all desire for isolation—such events give evidence in the social sphere of the extent to which active, practical self-definition issues from response to challenge rather than from the pursuit of an ideal or from adherence to some ultimate laws. In the case of individuals we are no less aware of the way in which opportunity on the one hand, limiting events on the other, form the matrix in which the self defines itself by the nature of its responses.

Perhaps this becomes especially evident in the case of suffering, a subject to which academic ethical theory, even theological ethics, usually pays little attention. Yet everyone with any experience of life is aware of the extent to which the characters of people he has known have been given their particular forms by the sufferings through which they have passed. But it is not simply what has happened to them that has defined them; their responses to what has happened to them have been of even greater importance, and these responses have been shaped by their interpretations of what they suffered. It may be possible to deal with the ethics of suffering by means of the general hypothesis of life's purposiveness; however when we do so there is much that we must leave out of consideration. For it is part of the meaning of suffering that it is that which cuts athwart our purposive movements. It represents the denial from beyond ourselves of our movement toward pleasure; or it is the frustration of our movement toward self-realization or toward the actualization of our potentialities. Because suffering is the exhibition of the presence in our existence of that which is not under our control, or of the intrusion into our self-legislating existence of an activity operating under another law than ours, it cannot be brought adequately within the spheres of teleological and deontological ethics, the ethics of man-the-maker, or man-the-citizen. Yet it is in the response to suffering that many and perhaps all men, individually and in their groups, define themselves, take on character, develop their ethos. And their responses are functions of their interpretation of what is happening to them as well as of the action upon them. It is unnecessary to multiply illustrations from history and experience of the actuality and relevance of the approach to man's self-conduct that begins with neither purposes nor laws but with responses; that begins with the question, not about the self as it is in itself, but as it is in its response-relations to what is given with it and to it. This question is already implied, for example, in the primordial action of parental guidance: "What is the fitting thing? What is going on in the life of the child?"

In summary of the foregoing argument we may say that purposiveness seeks to answer the question: "What shall I do?" by raising as prior the question: "What is my goal, ideal, or telos?" Deontology tries to answer the moral query by asking, first of all: "What is the law and what is the first law of my life?" Responsibility, however, proceeds in every moment of decision and choice to inquire: "What is going on?" If we use value terms then the differences among the three approaches may be indicated by the terms, the *good*, the *right,* and the *fitting;* for teleology is concerned always with the highest good to which it subordinates the right; consistent deontology is concerned with the right, no matter what may happen to our goods; but for the ethics of responsibility the *fitting* action, the one that fits into a total interaction as response and as anticipation of further response, is alone conducive to the good and alone is right.

The idea of responsibility, if it is to be made useful for the understanding of our self-action, needs to be brought into mind more clearly than has been done by these preliminary references to its uses in past theory and in common experience. Our definition should not only be as clear as we can make it; it should, if possible, be framed without the use of symbols referring to the other great ideas with which men have tried to understand their acts and agency. Only so will it be possible for us to develop a relatively precise instrument for self-understanding and also come to an understanding of the instrument's possibilities and limitations.

The first element in the theory of responsibility is the idea of *response*. All action, we now say, including what we rather indeterminately call moral action, is response to action upon us. We do not, however, call it the action of a self or moral action unless it is response to *interpreted* action upon us. All actions that go on within the sphere of our bodies, from heartbeats to knee jerks, are doubtless also reactions, but they do not fall within the domain of self-actions if they are not accompanied and infused, as it were, with interpretation. Whatever else we may need to say about ourselves in defining ourselves, we shall need, apparently, always to say that we are characterized by awareness and that this awareness is more or less that of an intelligence which identifies, compares, analyzes, and relates events so that they come to us not as brute actions, but as understood and as having meaning. Hence though our eyelids may react to the light with pure reflex, the self responds to it as *light,* as something interpreted, understood, related. But, more complexly, we interpret the things that force themselves upon us as parts of wholes, as related and as symbolic of larger meanings. And these large patterns of interpretation we employ seem to determine—though in no mechanical way—our responses to action upon us. We cannot understand international events, nor can we act upon each other as nations, without constantly interpreting the meaning of each other's actions. Russia and the United States confront each other not as those who are reflexively reacting to the manufacture of bombs and missiles, the granting of loans, and the making of speeches; but rather as two communities that are interpreting each other's actions and doing so with the aid of ideas about what is in the other's mind. So Americans try to understand Russia's immediate actions as expressions of the Communist or the Russian mind, which is the hidden part of the overt action, and we make our responses to the alien action in accordance with our interpretation of it as symbolic of a larger, an historic whole. The process of interpretation and response can be followed in all the public encounters of groups with each other. When we think of the relations of managers and employees we do not simply ask about the ends each group is consciously pursuing nor about the self-legislated laws they are obeying but about the way they are responding to each other's actions in accordance with their interpretations. Thus actions of labor unions may be understood better when we inquire less about what ends they are seeking and more about what ends they believe the managers to be seeking in all managerial actions. One must not deny the element of purposiveness in labor and in management, yet in their reactions to each other it is the interpretation each side has of the other's goals that may be more important than its definition of its own ends. Similarly in all the interactions of large groups with each other, law and duty seem to have a larger place in the interpretation of the other's conduct to which response is being made than they have in the immediate guidance of the agent's response. We use the idea of law less as a guide to our own conduct than as a way of predicting what the one will do to whom we are reacting or who will react to us. When lawyers try to discover under what law the judge will make his decisions, they are doing something akin to what we do in all our group relations; as Catholics or Protestants, also, we act less with an eye to our own law than to the other's action under his law, as we understand that law.

The point so illustrated by reference to groups applies to us as individuals. We respond as we interpret the meaning of actions upon us. The child's character may be formed less, the psychologists lead us to believe, by the injunctions and commandments of parents than by the child's interpretation of the attitudes such commandments are taken to express. The inferiority and superiority feelings, the aggressions, guilt feelings, and fears with which men encounter each other, and which do not easily yield to the commandment of neighbor-love, are dependent on their interpretations of each other's attitudes and valuations. We live as responsive beings not only in the social but also in the natural world where we interpret the natural events that affect us—heat and cold, storm and fair weather, earthquake and tidal wave, health and sickness, animal and plant—as living-giving and death-dealing. We respond to these events in accordance with our interpretation. Such interpretation, it need scarcely be added, is not simply an affair of our conscious, and rational, mind but also of the deep memories that are buried within us, of feelings and intuitions that are only partly under our immediate control.

This, then, is the second element in responsibility, that it is not only responsive action but responsive in accordance with our *interpretation* of the question to which answer is being given. In our responsibility we attempt to answer the question: "What shall I do?" by raising as the prior question: "What is going on?" or "What is being done to me?" rather than "What is my end?" or "What is my ultimate law?" A third element is *accountability*—a word that is frequently defined by recourse to legal thinking but

that has a more definite meaning, when we understand it as referring to part of the response pattern of our self-conduct. Our
actions are responsible not only insofar as they are reactions to
interpreted actions upon us but also insofar as they are made in
anticipation of answers to our answers. An agent's action is like
a statement in a dialogue. Such a statement not only seeks to meet,
as it were, or to fit into, the previous statement to which it is an
answer, but is made in anticipation of reply. It looks forward as
well as backward; it anticipates objections, confirmations, and cor-
rections. It is made as part of a total conversation that leads forward and is to have meaning as a whole. Thus a political action,
in this sense, is responsible not only when it is responsive to a prior
deed but when it is so made that the agent anticipates the reactions
to his action. So considered, no action taken as an atomic unit is
responsible. Responsibility lies in the agent who stays with his
action, who accepts the consequences in the form of reactions and
looks forward in a present deed to the continued interaction. From
this point of view we may try to illuminate the question much
debated in modern times of the extent to which a person is to be
held socially accountable for his acts. In terms of responsibility
the question is simply this: "To whom and in what way ought a
society through its courts and other agencies respond?" If a homi-
cide has taken place, is the only one to whom there is to be reaction the killer himself, or is there to be response also to the society
in which he acted as a reactor? Further, is the reaction to the individual criminal agent to be reaction guided by purely legal thinking, which interprets him solely as an unobedient and perhaps a
self-legislating being, or is it to be informed by a larger interpretation of his conduct—one which takes into account other dimensions of his existence as a self? Is the criminal to be dealt with as
a self who can anticipate reactions to his actions and so be acted
upon as a potentially responsive person, or is the social reaction
to him to be confined to his antisocial physical body only and he

be regarded as a being that cannot learn to respond with interpretation and anticipation? Is education, psychiatry, or only incarceration the fitting response?

This third element in responsibility—the anticipation of reaction to our reaction—has brought us within view of what at least for the present seems to be its fourth and final significant component, namely *social solidarity*. Our action is responsible, it appears, when it is response to action upon us in a continuing discourse or interaction among beings forming a continuing society. A series of responses to disconnected actions guided by disconnected interpretations would scarcely be the action of a self but only of a series of states of mind somehow connected with the same body— though the sameness of the body would be apparent only to an external point of view. Personal responsibility implies the continuity of a self with a relatively consistent scheme of interpretations of what it is reacting to. By the same token it implies continuity in the community of agents to which response is being made. There could be no responsible self in an interaction in which the reaction to one's response comes from a source wholly different from that whence the original action issued. This theme we shall need to develop more fully in the second lecture.

The idea or pattern of responsibility, then, may summarily and abstractly be defined as the idea of an agent's action as response to an action upon him in accordance with his interpretation of the latter action and with his expectation of response to his response; and all of this is in a continuing community of agents.

The idea of the moral life as the responsible life in this sense not only has affinities with much modern thinking but it also offers us, I believe, a key—not *the* key—to the understanding of that Biblical ethos which represents the historic norm of the Christian life. In the past many efforts have been made to understand the ethos of the Old and New Testaments with the aid of the teleological theory and its image of man-the-maker. Thus the thinking of the lawgivers and prophets, of Jesus Christ and the apostles, has been set before us in the terms of a great idealism. Sometimes the ideal has been described as that of the vision of God, sometimes as perfection, sometimes as eternal happiness, sometimes as a harmony of all beings, or at least of all men, in a kingdom of God. Each of these interpretations has been buttressed by collections of proof texts, and doubtless much that is valid about the Bible and about the Christian life which continues the Scriptural ethos has been said within the limits of this interpretation. But much that is in Scriptures has been omitted by the interpreters who followed this method, and much material of another sort—the eschatological, for instance—has had to be rather violently wrenched out of its context or laid aside as irrelevant in order to make the Scriptures speak in this fashion about the self. At all times, moreover, but particularly among the German interpreters in whom the Kantian symbolism holds sway, the deontological interpretation of man the obedient legislator has been used not only as the key to Biblical interpretation but for the definition of the true Christian life. For Barth and Bultmann alike in our times, not to speak of most interpreters of the Old Testament, the ethics of the Bible, and Christian ethics too, is the ethics of obedience. How to interpret Christian freedom and what to make of eschatology within this framework has taxed the ingenuity of the interpreters severely. Bultmann has transformed eschatology into existentialism in order to maintain an ethics of radical obedience; Barth has had to transform the law into a form of the gospel and the commandment into permission in order to reconcile the peculiarity of gospel ethos with deontological thinking. There is doubtless much about law, commandment, and obedience in the Scriptures. But the use of this pattern of interpretation does violence to what we find there.

If now we approach the Scriptures with the idea of responsibility we shall find, I think, that the particular character of this ethics can be more fully if not wholly adequately interpreted. At the critical junctures in the history of Israel and of the early Christian community the decisive question men raised was not "What is the goal?" nor yet "What is the law?" but "What is happening?" and then "What is the fitting response to what is happening?" When an Isaiah counsels his people, he does not remind them of the law they are required to obey nor yet of the goal toward which they are directed but calls to their attention the intentions of God present in hiddenness in the actions of Israel's enemies. The question he and his peers raise in every critical moment is about the interpretation of what is going on, whether what is happening be, immediately considered, a drought or the invasion of a foreign army, or the fall of a great empire. Israel is the people that is to see and understand the action of God in everything that happens and to make a fitting reply. So it is in the New Testament also. The God to whom Jesus points is not the commander who gives laws but the doer of small and of mighty deeds, the creator of sparrows and clother of lilies, the ultimate giver of blindness and of sight, the ruler whose rule is hidden in the manifold activities of plural agencies but is yet in a way visible to those who know how to interpret the signs of the times.

It will not do to say that the analysis of all our moral life in general and of Biblical ethics in particular by means of the idea of responsibility offers us an absolutely new way of understanding man's ethical life or of constructing a system of Christian ethics. Actuality always extends beyond the patterns of ideas into which we want to force it. But the approach to our moral existence as selves, and to our existence as Christians in particular, with the aid of this idea makes some aspects of our life as agents intelligible in a way that the teleology and deontology of traditional thought cannot do.

Some special aspects of life in responsibility are to occupy us in the succeeding lectures. In none of them shall I take the deontological stance, saying, "We *ought* to be responsible"; nor yet the ideal, saying, "The *goal* is responsibility"; but I shall simply ask that we consider our life of response to action upon us with the question in mind, "To whom or what am I responsible and in what community of interaction am I myself?"

2

Responsibility in Society

It is probably no accident that the idea of responsibility has come into view as a major pattern for self-understanding in the modern period of human history when our attention has been directed so strongly to the social character of all human life. There seems to be something rather individualistic about that conception of the self as agent which is connected with the image of man-the-maker. To be sure, this self does not form only its own life to accord with an ideal; as political leader devising the constitution of a society and administering it, or as educator assisting others to realize their entelecheia, the self-making agent is not a lonely self. Yet it understands itself as existing primarily in relation to ideas and ideals. It defines itself as rational, living in the symbiosis of reason with its objects, be they Platonic ideas, Aristotelian entelechies, scientific theories, or common-sense facts. When I so define myself as rational I make not only an observation about myself but also a choice. I tend to say that what is most important in me is that activity of understanding and knowing which is directed toward the general in the particular, toward the formal, measurable, and comparable in all occasions. I decide, as it were, in this self-definition that I will undertake to bring everything else within me—affective and emotive, unconscious as well as conscious reactions to other beings—into relation to my rational life, that is, to my existence in the presence of ideas or patterns or universals. In this situation I acknowledge a relation to other rational beings but my connection with them is a function of my relation to the objects of reason. First I know the objects of reason and only secondarily do I acknowledge other knowers. I may even raise the question of my ability to know other minds at all. I have a relation to their idea-content but no direct relation to the personal activity directed toward such ideas or to me as knower.

As practical agent actualizing ideas in human existence, man-the-maker can measure his achievement by comparison with the idea; he can judge the shortcomings or the successes of his endeavors; but unless he introduces an element for which his idea of himself makes no real room, he cannot speak of accountability for success or failure. Usually he does introduce some such notion of response to him and his work by other selves, but it seems to represent a surd in his thinking.

The image of man as self-legislator may seem to bear a less individualistic stamp. The law to which I consent, or which I give to myself, or against which I protest in the name of some higher law, is law of my society or for my society. In obedience to the law or in respect for it I am associated with other selves; indeed the others may be regarded as the authors of the law. Yet in this self-conception of moral man other selves also remain secondary. This man lives as moral self in the presence of law first of all, not of other selves. What is over against him as that which limits and attracts him is a commandment, a demand, a requirement. His relation to other selves is a relation under the law. They may be representatives of the law, enforcers of law, or in their obedience to it may command respect; but his first relation is to the law and not to other persons. Hence when I understand myself with this idea in mind my conscience appears to me to be the center of the self. I decide in-so defining the self that I will respect the conscience in myself and others as the most valuable element in selfhood, but the knowledge present in this conscience is knowledge of law and of myself in relation to law, not knowledge of other selves, or of myself in relation to those selves.

Now, however, there has come into view a new aspect of our self-existence and with it a possibility of new emphasis in practical self-definition. Without obscuring the fact that the self exists as rational being in the presence of ideas, or exists as moral being in the presence of mores and laws, this view holds in the center of attention the fundamentally social character of selfhood. To be a self in the presence of other selves is not a derivative experience but primordial. To be able to say that I am I is not an inference from the statement that I think thoughts nor from the statement that I have a law-acknowledging conscience. It is, rather, the acknowledgment of my existence as the counterpart of another self. The exploration of this dimension of self-existence has taken place in many areas of modern man's thinking; many lines of inquiry have converged on the recognition that the self is fundamentally social, in this sense that it is a being which not only knows itself in relation to other selves but exists as self only in that relation.

Among the lines of reflection which have led to this result is the one of social psychology. In America the work of George Horton Cooley, of George Herbert Mead, of Harry Stack Sullivan, and many others has led to the understanding that the self is a being which comes to knowledge of itself in the presence of other selves and that its very nature is that of a being which lives in response to other selves. The distinguishing characteristic of a *self*, Mead points out, following a long tradition, is that it is a being which is an object to itself, something we cannot say of bodies or even of minds as minds. Self is a *reflexive* word and points to the reflexive fact.—But how is it possible that a being can become an object to itself? Only, Mead argues, through dialogue with others. To be a being that is an object to itself is possible genetically and actually only as I take toward myself the attitude of other selves, see myself as seen, hear myself as heard, speak to myself as spoken to. "The self," he writes, "as that which can be an object to itself is essentially a social structure, and it arises in social experience. After a self has arisen, it in a certain sense provides for itself its social experiences, and so we can conceive of an absolutely solitary self. But it is impossible to conceive of a self arising outside of social experience."[1] Even that absolutely solitary self, we might add, is solitary only in a physical sense. As a self it engages in its lonely debates only in the presence of remembered or expected other selves present to its mind in memory or imagination.

The social psychology of G. H. Mead and his successors was developed in the context of evolutionary, biocentric, and behavioristic thinking, but a group of men with very different general orientations has been led to similar results. Among them Martin Buber is the best known.[2] In his existentialist reflections he has come upon the primordial character of "I-Thou" and "I-It" as prior to any atomic I or atomic object. He has called attention also to the difference between the I that is known and active in I-Thou dialectic and the I in the I-It interaction. Using Mead's language we might say that Buber points out how the I in I-It re-

---

[1] *The Social Psychology of George Herbert Mead,* ed. A. Strauss (Chicago: University of Chicago Press, 1956), p. 217.

[2] S. T. Coleridge ("Essay on Faith," *Works,* ed. Shedd [New York: Harper & Brothers, 1854], Vol. V) and Ludwig Feuerbach ("Grundsätze der Philosophie der Zukunft," §58–§63, *Werke* [Leipzig: Verlag von Otto Wigand, 1846], Vol. II) anticipated Buber.

lations is not a reflexive being. It does not know itself as known; it only knows; were it not for the accompanying I-Thou situation it would not know that it knows. It values but does not value itself or its evaluations. The I in I-It moves from within outward, as it were, and never turns back upon itself.

Other intellectual and practical movements of thought in the modern world have called attention to this social nature of selfhood which has been only at the periphery of theoretical and practical self-definitions in the past. The sociologists and cultural anthropologists who point out the difference between communities and contract societies and further maintain the priority of the former to the latter are on the same track as the social psychologists. The fundamental form of human association, it is seen, is not that contract society into which men enter as atomic individuals, making partial commitments to each other for the sake of gaining limited common ends or of maintaining certain laws; it is rather the face-to-face community in which unlimited commitments are the rule and in which every aspect of every self's existence is conditioned by membership in the interpersonal group. Hobbesian contract societies do indeed exist; they have been preceded, however, not by separate individuals, but by communities from which individuals only gradually distinguished themselves and whose influence they have never shaken off. To say the self is social is not to say that it finds itself in need of fellow men in order to achieve its purposes, but that it is born in the womb of society as a sentient, thinking, needful being with certain definitions of its needs and with the possibility of experience of a common world. It is born in society as mind and as moral being, but above all it is born in society as self.

The understanding of the self as social, living in response-relations to other selves, has been current in the realm of moral philosophy for a longer time than in these other fields of inquiry. The strange duality in man which manifests itself in the phenomenon of conscience had of course long been remarked by philosophers. Bishop Butler stated the common-sense understanding of the phenomenon when he wrote: "We are plainly constituted such sort of creatures as to reflect on our own nature. The mind can take a view of what passes within itself, its propensions, aversions, passions, affections. . . . In this survey it approves of one, disapproves of another and towards a third . . . is indifferent. . . . This principle in man by which he approves or disapproves his heart, temper and actions, is conscience." But Butler took the presence of conscience for granted, as though it required no further analysis.[3] Kant described the same duality with the use of his legal archetype imagery: "Every man has a conscience, and finds himself observed by an inward judge which threatens and keeps him in awe . . . and this power which watches over the laws within him is not something which he himself (arbitrarily) *makes,* but it is incorporated in his being. . . . Now this original intellectual and moral capacity, called *conscience,* has this peculiarity in it, that although its business is a business of man with himself, yet he finds himself compelled by his reason to transact it *as if* at the command of *another person.* For the transaction here is the conduct of a *trial (causa)* before a tribunal. But that he who is *accused* by his conscience should be conceived as *one* and *the same person* with the judge is an absurd conception of a judicial court. . . . Therefore in all duties the conscience of a man must regard *another* than himself as the judge of his actions, if it is to avoid self-contradiction. Now this other may be an actual or a merely ideal person which reason frames to itself."[4]

[3] Joseph Butler, *Works,* ed. W. E. Gladstone (Oxford: Clarendon Press, 1896), Vol. II, "Sermon I," pars. 7 and 8.

[4] *Kant's Critique of Practical Reason and Other Works on The Theory of Ethics,* ed. and trans. T. K. Abbott (London: Longmans, Green & Co. Ltd., 6th ed., 1927), pp. 321 f. ("as if" italicized by H.R.N.—Ed.).

I have quoted the passage at some length because it illustrates well the conflict of Kant's archetypal image of man under law with the actualities of the phenomenon he was trying to understand. There is no *"as if"* about this situation, Hume and Adam Smith maintain. Isolated reason does not, in order to be consistent with itself, invent another person. The experience of conscience is not *like* being judged by another person; it is indeed being judged by another, though the other is not immediately or symbolically and physically present to sense-experiencing man. Conscience is a function of my existence as a social being, always aware of the approvals and disapprovals of my action by my fellow men. "We can never survey our own sentiments and motives," Smith writes, "we can never form any judgment concerning them; unless we remove ourselves, as it were, from our own natural station, and endeavor to view them at a certain distance from us. But we can do this in no other way than by endeavouring to view them with the eyes of other people, or as other people are likely to view them. . . . We endeavour to examine our own conduct as we imagine any other fair and impartial spectator would examine it."[5] Adam Smith appealed to no *as if* thinking; he accepted the social character of moral man as fundamental.

This social theory of the conscience has had a long history from Hume's theory of social approval and disapproval to Freud's superego, Westermarck's theory of moral relativity and the latest variations on the theme in analysts' discussions of the logic of social moral language. The debate between defenders of a so-called "higher" or rationalist view of conscience and the social analysts of the phenomenon is much confused. In and of itself a social interpretation of conscience does not say anything about the rational or emotional character nor about the extent of that society in

[5] *The Theory of Moral Sentiments*, in L. A. Selby-Bigge, ed., *British Moralists, Selections from Writers Principally of the Eighteenth Century* (London: Oxford University Press, 1897), Vol. I, pp. 297-98.

which man is able to reflect on his own deeds, by viewing them with the eyes of others. It does not, in itself, deliver man to the tyranny of the approvals and disapprovals of any immediately given biologically existent group. But discounting the confusions that arise because the social principle is falsely identified with ideas of emotional or of provincial companions, we may rule out the "as ifs" of idealistic and rationalistic interpretations. When we judge our actions, approve and disapprove of ourselves, value and disvalue our evaluations, the situation is the same social situation in which we transcend ourselves by knowing ourselves as knowers. All this reflective life is life in relations to companions; it is I-Thou, I-You, existence. It is existence in response to action upon us by other selves.

II

THE SOCIAL understanding of *conscience* has brought into view an aspect of our self-existence that concentration on its pure I-Thou character tends to leave out of account. The self that judges itself, said Adam Smith, regards itself from the point of view of an impartial spectator. The approvals and disapprovals of others to which we respond in our moral life, as Westermarck believed, represent *disinterested* moral emotions. "Almost inseparable from the judgment that we pass on our own conduct seems to be the image of an impartial outsider who acts as our judge."[6] G. H. Mead substituted for the term "impartial spectator" "generalized other." "We assume the generalized attitude of the group, in the censor that stands at the door of our imagery and inner conversations, and in the affirmation of the laws and axioms of the universe of discourse. . . . Our thinking is an inner conversation in which we may be taking the roles of specific acquaintances over against

---

[6] Edward Westermarck, *Ethical Relativity* (New York: Harcourt, Brace & Co., 1932), p. 95.

ourselves, but usually it is with what I have termed the 'generalized other' that we converse . . ."[7]

The terms *"impartial* spectator" and *"generalized* other" seem to refer to unanalyzed and rather vague notions, which it may be possible to define somewhat more accurately. At least the attempt must be made. The self does not live—it is hard to see how it could—with any innate knowledge of its own continuity and self-identity in movement from one I-Thou relation to another. It lives rather in responsive relations to Thou's who on the one hand display constancy in their actions toward the self, and on the other live in constant response-relations to other Thou's and It's. I can respond to the action of the other, or anticipate his reaction to my action, only as I interpret his movements directed toward me. I respond to his action not as isolated event but as action in a context, as part of a larger pattern. That pattern to be sure has been discerned and learned in the course of many encounters. But apart from such interpretation, apart from the relating of the other's present action to a before and after, I could only react, not respond; or it may be better to say that in such a situation something, but not a continuing self, reacts to something, but not to a continuing Thou. In actual practice, however, the other and his actions are not atomic events or occasions to which atomic reactions are made; they are particular demonstrations of an enduring movement or particular parts of a continuous discourse. I live in the presence of, and in response to, a Thou who is not an isolated event but symbolic in his particularity of something general and constant. In the other I meet not a composite other but yet something general in the particular.

Beyond the constancy in the attitude of the Thou toward me there is now to be considered the constancy in his interactions with members of the community other than myself. When I speak I do

[7] *The Philosophy of the Present* (Chicago: Open Court Publishing Co., 1932), p. 190.

not address myself to a generalized other or to an impartial spectator but to particular selves in whose interactions with each other and with the objects of discourse there is a constancy on which I have learned to depend. When in the experience of conscience I judge my action from the point of view of another, I do not abstract some vague general figure from all the particular individuals who together constitute my society, but I refer to the constancies in the responses of individuals—a constancy which is presented, if nowhere else, at least in the constant meanings of a common language. The social self is never a mere I-Thou self but an I-*You* self, responding to a Thou that is a member of an interacting community. And in its interaction with others, constancies have been demonstrated which enable the self to interpret the action upon him. In referring to these constancies of behavior which enable one to interpret the action of the other upon the self, we seem to have re-established that idea of law that the Kantian moralists make their point of departure. Yet there is this difference, that when I view my life from the standpoint of its existence in responsibility I am not so much aware of law in the form of demand as of the action of other beings upon me in anticipated and predictable ways. In my responsive relations with others I am dealing not with laws but with men, though with men who are not atoms but members of a system of interactions. If law is present here it is present more in analogy to natural law in the modern or perhaps nineteenth-century sense than to obligatory, political law.

So the social self exists in responses neither to atomic other beings nor to a generalized other or impartial spectator but to others who as Thou's are members of a group in whose interactions constancies are present in such a way that the self can interpret present and anticipate future action upon it. It can respond to the meaning of present action because such action is a part of a total action, something which *means* the total action or derives its meaning from that whole. So my conscience represents not so much my awareness of the approvals and disapprovals of other individuals in isolation as of the ethos of my society, that is, of its mode of interpersonal interactions.

III

THE ANALYSIS of the self as responsive and responsible in its social character must, now, be taken a step further. The self existing as I-Thou being in the presence of Thou's that so interact as to form a relatively predictable society is led to respond in that situation not only to the Thou's and to the You but to that to which Thou's and the You respond. The dual character of my life in response has already come into view with the critique of the notion of a generalized other. When the Thou is present to me as a knower, it is present as the one that knows not only me but at least one other; and it knows me as knowing not only the Thou but something besides it. This encounter of I and Thou takes place, as it were, always in the presence of a third, from which I and Thou are distinguished and to which they also respond.

The triadic form of our life in response is perhaps most evident to us in that double relation to society and nature in which our knowing of natural events occurs. What I mean by nature in this connection is that large world of events and agencies that we regard as impersonal, as purely objective or thing-like in character. It is the congeries or system of those actualities, events and energies that we know but that we do not interpret as knowing us or knowing themselves. This system of the natural, however, is never present to us in isolation from the social companions who know it and us and themselves. I respond to natural events and do so as one who interprets them in their interrelations and meanings; but my interpretation seems never to be the result of my encounter with natural events alone. From childhood onward these occasions have been interpreted to me by companions who have been not only knowers of my self but of nature also. Through the medium of language, with its names and categories, its grammar and syntax, its logic, I have been introduced to the system of nature, that is, to the *system* of nature as *systematized* by society. I classify the events and find their meaning in their relations to each other but do so always with the aid of the a priori categories of my social, historical reason, derived from my companions. To them I look not only for the categorial schemes with which I organize and interpret natural events but also for the verification of my reports of my direct encounters with nature. Hence it is that the concept of nature has a history and that men respond to natural events in varying ways in different periods of social history, on the basis of their different interpretations.

When I respond to natural events I do so as a social being; on the other hand, when I respond to my companions I do so as one who is in response-relations to nature. I do not exist as responsive self in two separate spheres or in two distinct encounters—with the Thou on the one hand, with the It on the other; with society on the one hand, with nature on the other. I engage rather in a continuous dialogue in which there are at least these three partners—the self, the social companion, and natural events. As it is true that I encounter and interpret no natural event except as one who has been and will be in encounter with social companions—also related to such events—so it is true that I do not usually encounter and interpret the speech of companions except as one who lives in relation to nature and interprets their words as issuing out of a like relation. Communication between selves—except for those rare forms in which only I and Thou are involved, as in declarations of love and hate—is always explicitly or implicitly communication *about* something and that something must be a thing with which both social partners are in communication. Whether it belongs to the order of sensed qualities such as colors and sounds, or entities such as cats and chairs, or abstract realities such as numbers and ideas of conscience, or of quanta, or large totalities that are neither sensed nor abstract, such as nations and systems of nature, in any case communication between selves implies the presence of another duologue than the one between such selves. And conversely, there seems to be no interpretation and response to the world of It's, or of third-person beings, without the accompaniment of the I-Thou duologue.[8]

Since this is the situation, the self is never *wholly* dependent upon, as it is never *wholly* independent of, the Thou and the You. I am independent of the society in my interpretation of, and my response to, natural events to the extent that I have a direct relation to these events and can compare the social reason or the dominant pattern of interpretation with my experiences. But no one is so independent of his social culture that he can meet and interpret the events we call nature without some of the words, categories, and relations supplied by his society. The picture of the radical doubter who sits down before natural events like a little child to be freshly taught by them could be painted only by a generation which had made no study of little children, had paid little attention to the way in which language transmits interpretations, and knew nothing of the social, historical character of our knowledge of nature in general, of our art and our science in particular. But the opposite picture of the self as one which is so determined by the conventional views of its prescientific or scientific society that it cannot respond to natural events except in ordained fashion and with conventional symbols is no less an abstraction from the actuality of our existence. It must ignore for the sake of its dogma all that is personal and all that is novel, in scientific theory or in poetic vision or artistic reconstruction of natural phenomena.

The self before nature remains a social self, responding to other selves in all responses to nature. It is also an accountable self,

---

[8] A dialogue consists of at least two duologues.—Ed.

called upon by its companions to answer for its responses to nature. Responsiveness now becomes responsibility in the sense of accountability when response is made not to one being alone but to that being as related with the self to a third reality. That I am responsible in my reactions to the actions of natural forces upon me means first that I anticipate reaction to my action from natural force itself, as when I am tempted by the poisonous mushroom the appearance of which I have misinterpreted. It means, secondly, that I act in anticipation of response to my reaction from the side of my social companions who are related to the natural events and also to me and who verify or correct my interpretations of the natural. My action takes place as responsive and responsible in the midst of these interpretations and anticipations of reaction from both society and nature.

In this first illustration of the triadic character of the situation in which responsivity and responsibility occur, we have confined ourselves largely to communication about interpreted natural events. The responsible self appears in this connection as one who responds to nature and then is reacted to by other selves also responding to the natural event, as when the child calls a lamb a "kitty" and is corrected by its mother, or as when a scientist publishes his theory of the origin of species and awaits its verification, correction, and denial by fellow scientists, philosophers, theologians, and the community at large; or as when another scientist maintains the actuality of extrasensory perception and answers the massive social disbelief he encounters with independent certainty, yet as awaiting future social verification.

The responsive self, however, exists in another triadic, dialectical interaction. Traditionally we have distinguished this second situation from the first by saying that in it we exercise practical reason, while in the other we use speculative or observing reason. Useful and unavoidable as this distinction is, it tends to lead us somewhat astray by dissolving the unity of the self, somewhat as the similar, useful, but also misleading distinction between body and mind does. Equally serious has been the consequence that the separation has often led us to ignore the practical or ethical elements in our knowing as well as the observing, interpreting elements in our doing. Instead of distinguishing the two situations by reference to the subjective activity of reason as contemplative or practical, we have more recently tended to distinguish them by reference to their objects as *facts* and *values*. But it is notorious that it is difficult to give definite meaning to either of these words, or even to correlate them as designating species of one genus, for instance, of being. It may be that the general problem which we have tried to solve with the use of these two familiar distinctions can be brought to our attention in a slightly different perspective with this view of ourselves as responsible beings, though it remains doubtful whether the ultimate problem of the unity of the self can be solved by means of this approach entirely more satisfactorily than it has been by means of the older distinctions.

The second triadic situation in which we find ourselves responding and responsible is the one my countryman Josiah Royce has described with the aid of the idea of the cause. He sought to understand the moral life as primarily an affair of loyalty, a notion closely related to our notion of responsibility. Instead of thinking of man as realizer of ideals or as obedient to laws he saw him as one who comes to selfhood by committing himself to a cause. When a person is able to say, "For this cause was I born and therefore came I into the world," he has arrived at mature selfhood. Now in devotion to a cause—be it a nation or science or a religion or some simple duty—he finds himself associated with other loyalists to the same cause. The bond of loyalty is then a double bond, on the one hand to the companions, on the other to the cause. So the soldier's loyalty is an affair of faithfulness to his fellow soldiers, and to the cause, never to one of them alone. Leaving the idea of loyalty aside, for the moment, we note in

Royce's analysis the appearance of the triadic structure of responsibility in social existence in general. The patriot is related to his country as the cause and to his fellow citizens. He responds to the actions of his fellow citizens, their calls upon him for service, their criticisms, their praises, their approvals and disapprovals, as one who is also engaged in dialogue with his nation and looks to it, or its representatives, for ultimate praise and blame. In reaction to the present action of his companions, he anticipates the action upon him of that third and does his fitting act, that is, makes a response that fits into this continuing triadic interaction.

In other analyses of human self-conduct the third may appear as that reference group to which the self relates himself as he reacts to present challenges. He plays his various roles, as social psychologists point out, in meeting the challenges and expectations of his immediate fellow men by referring always to some prestige persons or societies with whom he identifies himself and of whom he asks —in interior dialogue at least—not only how they would act in his situation but how they would approve, disapprove, or correct his conduct and reaction to his companions.

IV

WHEN WE reflect about this third reality that is present to us in all our responses to our companions we note that it always has a double character. On the one hand it is something personal; on the other it contains within itself again a reference to something that transcends it or to which it refers. The generalized other or the impartial spectator of the empirical conscience is a knower and an evaluator, representing the community but also the community's cause. The law to which I refer in all questions of legal responsibility means both the administrators of my society's justice and the justice to which my society refers as lying beyond it. In the situation of the patriot, the third to whom he is related besides his co-patriots is a nation or country, but that country is not only a community of persons living and dead—heroes of the past and the future, founding fathers and historical posterity to whom appeal is made; it is always such a community plus that to which these representatives make their reference. This reference may be made with the use of the language of cause, as when we speak of democracy in America, or the true religion in old Spain, or communism in Russia. That cause, when analyzed, always shows again the double character of being something personal and something that transcends the persons. A democratic patriot in the United States, for instance, will carry on his dialogue with current companions, but as one who is also in relation to what his companions refer to—representatives of the community such as Washingtons, Jeffersons, Madisons, Lincolns, etc. Responsive to his companions he is also responsive to a transcendent reference group and thereby achieves a relative independence from his immediate associates. Insofar he has become not only a responsive but also an accountable self. But now the transcendent reference group—these founding fathers, for instance, encountered in memory and these representatives of the community in a later time encountered in anticipation—refer beyond themselves. They are persons who stand for something and represent something. They represent not the community only but what the community stands for. Ultimately we arrive in the case of democracy at a community which refers beyond itself to humanity and which in doing so seems to envisage not only representatives of the human community as such but a universal society and a universal generalized other, Nature and Nature's God.

When we educate children to become responsible citizens in Western societies we seek to relate them to such founding fathers and the great ideas of their histories. We do not think that they will become responsible if they are related simply to their fellow citizens. They must also have direct connection with their country and its cause—what it stands for—so that they can interpret the actions of their fellow citizens in the context of the national intention; so that they will not be subject to the tyranny of the immediate instance and the present moment. When we do this and lead them to read in America, for instance, the Declaration of Independence we introduce them to a company of national representatives who act as accountable for their actions, who make their statement out of a "decent respect for the opinions of mankind." But this mankind, or its representatives, is regarded by them as one that is related to an ultimate community in which all men are equal and are related also to "the Supreme judge of the world."

I might more readily have drawn my illustrations of the triadic situation in which we are responsible from the church but have hesitated to do so, since I am undertaking in these prolegomena to Christian ethics to abstract from life in the church as I try to develop instruments for the believer's self-understanding. It seems evident that as I respond in the church I respond to my companions, that is, to the fellowship of the members of the church. They have taught me the language, the words, the logic of religious discourse. But the discourse is not about them, it is about a third. To these fellow members I am challenged to be faithful, but not otherwise than in faithfulness to the common cause. That common cause is represented to me by the prophets and apostles. Yet they point beyond themselves. And even when I find that I can be responsible in the church only as I respond to Jesus Christ, I discover in him one who points beyond himself to the cause to which he is faithful and in faithfulness to which he is faithful to his companions—not the companions encountered in the church, but in the world to which the Creator is faithful, which the Creator has made his cause.

To the monotheistic believer for whom all responses to his companions are interrelated with his responses to God as the ultimate person, the ultimate cause, the center of universal community, there seem to be indications in the whole of the responsive, accountable life of men of a movement of self-judgment and self-guidance which cannot come to rest until it makes its reference to a universal other and a universal community, which that other both represents and makes his cause. It is not my intention to contend here for the validity of a new form of the moral argument for God. I only register this observation, that these social theories of the moral life as responsible are neither just to the empirical facts nor consistent with their fundamental idea if they stop such analysis at the point of reference to the ethos, or the judging actions of a closed society to which a man responds in all his responses to his companions. These societies are not more self-contained than are the individuals that refer to them; these moral languages in which social judgments are enshrined are no more self-elucidating than are languages about nature. The societies that judge or in which we judge ourselves are self-transcending societies. And the process of self-transcendence or of reference to the third beyond each third does not come to rest until the total community of being has been involved.

When we approach man's existence as self-administrative with the aid of the idea of responsibility, we are caught up in the same movement toward the universal in which the other approaches to ethics, that is, teleology and deontology, find themselves involved. In teleological ethics we move toward asking as our final question: "What idea is being realized in the totality of being?" We ask: "What is the Form of the Good that is the form of the whole?" In deontology we eventually ask: "What is the universal form of the law?" And now in *cathēkontic* ethics, or the ethics of the fitting, we find ourselves led to the notion of universal responsibility, that is, of a life of responses to actions which is always qualified by our interpretation of these actions as taking place in a *universe,* and by the further understanding that there will be a response to our actions by representatives of universal community, or by the generalized other who is universal, or by an impartial spectator who regards our actions from a universal point of view, whose impartiality is that of loyalty to the universal cause.

This situation in ethics has its parallel, I believe, in science which beyond all generalities seeks the universal in the particular and operates as with universal intent. It does not proceed from a known or defined universal to the particular as an earlier rationalism did, but moving toward the particular it seeks in it the pattern that is verifiable by other knowers; in seeking the relations of patterns to patterns it seeks what is verifiable in universal knowing. Though science does not undertake to know the universal, it seeks to interpret each particular occasion by reference to more general patterns so that the movement is toward the universal. It operates with universal intent. And in the appeal for verification, or in accountability as it figures in our knowing, there is the same latent appeal to a universal knowing as in the movement of self-judgment there is the appeal to a universal evaluating.

In the midst of our social responsibilities, it is true, we do not follow out to their universal end the references we make to those third representatives of more inclusive communities and causes. Man-the-maker does not follow out to *the* end the question of the ultimate idea toward which each realized idea is only *an* end. Man the self-legislator does not in his practical thinking always move toward the *universal* form of the maxim that he adopts as the rule of his present action. But in the critical moments we do ask about the ultimate causes and the ultimate judges and are led to see that our life in response to action upon us, our life in anticipation of response to our reactions, takes place within a society whose boundaries cannot be drawn in space, or time, or extent of interaction, short of a whole in which we live and move and have our being.

The responsible self is driven as it were by the movement of the social process to respond and be accountable in nothing less than a universal community.

Whether this movement toward universal community seems evident to any other than a monotheistic point of view is a question I need not debate, since this essay is an effort at self-understanding in the community of believing men, who yet understand unbelief very well because they share in it so largely. When this monotheistic believer tries to understand his own life, he finds that it is a life lived less under universal law and less in pursuit of a universal ideal than a life of responsibility in universal community. And it seems to him that in unacknowledged ways those responsible men he encounters who call themselves unbelievers are acting similarly, as if they needed to interpret all events and their reactions as occurrences in universe.

Responsibility, however, is exercised in time, as well as in society, and to that theme we shall attend next.

3

THE RESPONSIBLE SELF IN TIME AND HISTORY

THE RECOGNITION that the I, this acting self, is a time-full and historical being does not seem to be of first importance in those ways of thinking about our activity which employ the archetypal figures of man-the-maker or of obedient, law-consenting man. Man-the-maker does indeed reckon on the span of future time available to him for the actualization of what is potential in his material. The teleologist is always also something of an eschatologist who takes into view his *finis* as well as his goal. The Epicurean with his ideal of a quiet, undisturbed life, devoid of the perturbations of extreme pleasure no less than of pain, presents to men a shrewd plan for an existence that must end with death. It is the sad philosophy, as Gilbert Murray has called it, of those who know how short time is; they do not undertake to build what they cannot finish or to employ those materials fit only for use in a structure that would require many generations or unlimited time for its completion. The spiritual idealist with everlasting time ahead of him may differ from the Epicurean more because of his future prospect than because he thinks of tending the soul rather than the life that is sensitive to pleasure and pain. The social idealist who sees man as a political animal, participating in the life of the group, finds the shortness or the indefinite extension of the social future important in projecting his goals and making his plans. There are five-year teleologists and teleologists of infinite progress. Thus man's time as future does enter into the practical assessment of potentiality and into the definition of the ideal by those who see him as man-the-maker. But of the critical present they seem hardly aware and the past seems to be of little moment in this way of thinking about our action. This may be the reason why there is so little reference in most academic thought of this type to such subjects as sin and guilt. One twentieth-century representative of man-the-maker ethics, Nicolai Hartmann, does indeed give some attention to the social, historical past as the scene in which the great moral ideas have been gradually disclosed. The past of the individual also has some significance for him in the form of guilt; yet guilt regarded from this point of view is something that man must simply bear; in bearing it, resolutely indeed, he realizes better the ideal of his personal existence. So even for Hartmann time does not affect either the ideas or their actualizers in any very significant fashion.

In the formalistic ethics of man as obedient to law—the doer of the right—time and history seem even less important than in teleology. In Kant, the most consistent representative of this way of defining and ruling the self, time is a form of sense perception only; it is even less relevant to the activity of the pure practical reason than to that of the pure speculative reason; ". . . when the law of our intelligible [supersensible] existence (the moral law) is in question," he writes, "reason recognizes no distinction of time, and only asks whether the event belongs to me, as my act, and then always morally connects the same feeling with it, whether it has happened just now or long ago."[1] And again: ". . . existence in time is a mere sensible mode of representation belonging to thinking beings in the world, and consequently does not apply to them as things in themselves . . ."[2] In connection with his doctrine of the *summum bonum,* to be sure, immortal existence does come into consideration as the postulate reason makes of the availability of time in which to realize virtue and of time in which happiness may be added to virtue. But in Kant this is mostly afterthought; it is the adjustment of a rigorously logical system, based on self-legislation only, to the practical needs of a man who, though essentially intelligible being, is a sense-being also. Man-the-citizen stands in the presence of a pure supertemporal law valid for his reason as a pure, nontemporal reason. Because he is a desiring sense-being as well as rational, he doubtless yearns toward the future, but in his innermost rational self he does not take it into account. For Kant and the Kantians, as for Victor Hugo, "the future is not one of my concerns," nor is the past.[3] Kierkegaard, rigorous developer of the idea of Kant's second critique that he was, tended to concentrate all the meaning of personal existence into the moment. His followers, the extreme existentialists, define man in his freedom as one who newly creates, chooses, and defines himself in every present, though now he stands alone without even a universal law before him. With them the subtraction from existing man of his time-fullness, his past and future and his historicity, has gone as far as it seems possible to go.

Yet the phenomenal self I know in being known, the selves my companions reveal to me, the self that knows itself as it acts, de-

[1] *Kant's Critique of Practical Reason,* etc., ed. Abbott, p. 192.
[2] *Ibid.,* p. 196.
[3] Cf. Kant, *Religion within the Limits of Reason Alone,* trans. T. M. Greene and H. H. Hudson (Chicago: Open Court Publishing Co., 1934; Harper Torchbooks, 1960), e.g. Bk. II, Sec. One, c.

fines, decides, chooses, or otherwise moves out from itself, is time-full in ways of which teleology and deontology seem unaware. It is a self that is always in the present to be sure, always in the moment, so that the very notion of the *present* is probably unthinkable apart from some implicit reference to a self. *I* and *now* belong together somewhat as do I and Thou and I and It do. But only from the point of view of an external observer who abstracts from personal existence is this now a point in clock-time between the no-longer and the not-yet. For the time-full self the past and the future are not the no-longer and the not-yet; they are extensions of the present. They are the still-present and the already-present. My past is with me now; it is in my present as conscious and unconscious memory; it is here now as habits of behavior, of speech and thought, as ways of cutting up and dividing into shapes and forms the great mass of impressions made on my senses by the energies assailing them from without. My interpersonal past also is with me in all my present meetings with other selves. It is there in all my love and guilt. The self does not leave its past behind as the moving hand of a clock does; its past is inscribed into it more deeply than the past of geologic formations is crystallized in their present form. As for the future, the not-yet, it is present in my now in expectations and anxieties, in anticipations and commitments, in hopes and fears. To be a self is to live toward the future and to do so not only in the form of purposiveness, but also of expectation, anticipation, anxiety, and hope. Past, present, and future are dimensions of the active self's time-fullness. They are always with it from the moment it has realized that "I am I." Whatever else the much commented upon continuity of the self in time may mean, this much must be included: the self existing always in a now is one that knows itself as having been and as going into existence and into encounter.

II

THIS EXISTENCE as time-full is existence in encounter, in challenge and in response. To be in the present is to be in *compresence* with what is not myself. When abstraction is made from all compresence, as in moments of mystic absorption, the sense of the now disappears; present in this instance could only mean the presence of the mystic to some other nonmystic self, aware of him as compresent. But in the mystic's moment of absorption the self as well as past, present, and future seem to disappear. On the other hand we are most aware of our existence in the moment, in the now, when we are radically acted upon by something from without, when we are under the necessity of meeting a challenge with an action of our own, as is the case in every important decision. This radical sense of existence now is the sense of being compresent with those others or those actions that have not been in our past, at least not in the way they now are. For the most part our now's succeed each other without calling attention to themselves because they are the now's of routine, of repetition in encounter with familiar others and well-known actions. The keener sense of the moment arrives on the D-days of our personal and social life; and these are present moments in which we are *compresent* with a not-ourself in threatening or promising form.

The past that we carry with us is also an affair of compresences. The self remembers itself but remembers itself in encounter with others. It remembers its parents and their actions upon it and its responses to them. It remembers with pain those of its reactions that excited the response of disapproval and recalls with pleasure past approvals. Its past is present also in the slowly acquired habits of response toward certain continually or frequently compresent It's and Thou's. The past is present in the familiar language learned in childhood, which brings before the self the images or ideas of previously compresent beings. It is present in the repressed emotions that were not allowed to come to the surface in certain situations. This whole past, in its many still unexplored forms, which the self brings into its present, is a past of responses to other beings and of actions upon them in expectation of their reactions.

So it is also with the future. I enter it with my plans and with my self-legislated laws, my resolutions. But every New Year's Day is more a day of expectation, prediction, hope, and anxiety than a day of resolves. For this future into which the self forever advances is also an affair of encounter, of action and response, of meeting with compresences. This present is the time of preparation to meet the actions on me that I foresee, hope for, or fear. So far as it is the future of compresence with familiar, constant actualities it scarcely modifies my present. I shall expect the sun to rise day after day, food to be provided meal after meal; I expect the mechanisms of nature and of society to present to me in my future those actualities to which I shall be able to make my habitual responses. That uncritical future is also one of compresences, but the future which makes a *difference* to my present action is the future of impending questions to be addressed to me to which I do not know the answer, of actions upon me by new compresences, or of unfamiliar actions upon me by those who have been present to me in my past. It is the future, too, in which I dread or hope for responses from my companions to actions of mine that lie in my past. So my guilt as well as my anxiety are functions of this existence in encounter with the compresent in time-full existence. I experience my guilt not as a relation to the law or to an ideal, but to my companions. And I experience it not as my relation to timeless being but as relation to a continuous interaction that has gone on and will go on through a long time.

III

THIS time-full self in encounter responds to actions upon it in accordance with interpretations that are themselves time-full. Not with timeless ideas, recollected in Platonic recall of the soul's participations in the eternal; not with timeless laws of never-changing nature or of a pure human, unhistorical reason, does the self come to its present encounters. It comes rather with images and patterns of interpretation, with attitudes of trust and suspicion, accumulated in its biographical and historical past. It comes to its meetings with the Thou's and It's with an a priori equipment that is the heritage of its personal and social past; and it responds to the action of these others in accordance with the interpretations so made possible. The remembered images are the product not, in the first place, of its own past encounters but of a society which has taught it a language with names and explicit or implicit metaphors and with an implicit logic. With the aid of that language the self has learned to divide up the continuum of its experiences into separate entities, to distinguish things and persons, processes in nature and movements in society. Hence its responses in the present to encountered Thou's and It's are guided largely by the remembered, a priori patterns. It seeks to interpret each new occasion by assimilating it to an old encounter, and it tends to respond to the newly present in the way it had learned to answer its apparent counterparts in the past. The responsive, interpreting self is highly conservative not because it loves the past but because its interpretative equipment binds it to the past. The categories of its historical reason largely determine what it can now know and how it will now respond.

However, it is not the social past only that we bring into our present but also our personal, private remembrance of our previous encounters and responses. The tones of fear and guilt and joy that were attached to past meetings, to past actions on us by others, and to our past responses are attached now also to actions and interpretations in the present as we encounter those beings who are like the Thou's and It's of our remembrance. We interpret not only with the aid of our historic images but in trust and distrust, with fear and joy, with the aid of our remembered feelings, whether the memory be conscious or unconscious.

Our interpretations of present actions upon us are made with reference to the future as well as to the past. This present other being that challenges me or aids me or otherwise acts upon me is one that I expect or do not expect to meet in my future. I may interpret its action as casual, requiring no answer, because I shall never meet it again. Its action is held to be predictive or prophetic of nothing. On the other hand it may be pregnant with potentialities and my response must be fitting, as one of a series of interactions that will culminate in some near or far future. Or otherwise, my reactions to the beings I encounter in the present is one that disvalues them as unimportant, because I am preparing to meet more valued or more significant beings in my future. I pass by on the other side of the road, as I meet my appointments in earthly or heavenly Jerusalems, in mundane or otherworldly Gehennas. Regarding my action as directed toward future encounter, I fail frequently to note that it is also an action of response to beings I encounter in the present, though it is an action of ignoring.

Thus our responsive actions have the character of fittingness or unfittingness. We seek to make them fit into a process of interaction. The questions we raise about them are not only those of their rightness or wrongness, their goodness or badness, but of their fitness or unfittingness in the total movement, the whole conversation. We seek to have them fit into the whole as a sentence fits into a paragraph in a book, a note into a chord in a movement in a symphony, as the act of eating a common meal fits into the lifelong companionship of a family, as the decision of a statesman fits into the ongoing movement of his nation's life with other nations, or as the discovery of a scientific verifact fits into the history of science. But whether they fit into the actual process, that is another story.

IV

So WE have come upon the great question of the total context in which we respond and by means of which we interpret all the specific actions upon us. What is the time span in which our responsive actions take place? Into what history do we make these actions of ours fit? For the most part it seems that responsive man has short spans of time in view. He acts in the light of brief pasts and brief futures; and yet these short periods of his one- and four- and five-year plans are surrounded by his sense of his lifetime, of his social and his human history. Hence his interpretations of present events are always modified by the larger contexts in which they are placed. The student superficially interpreted may seem to us to act in a present that has no past reaching beyond his joining of the academic society and no future beyond his leaving it. Yet we know after brief inquiry that this is an illusion. His lifetime in a larger community and the lifetime of that larger community are present to him in all his responses, as they are in the action of teachers upon him. Man responding in the present is interpreting what acts upon him as historical being, being in time.

Those observers of our condition do not seem far wrong who say that for the most part if not universally we respond to present occasions in anxiety, as men whose ultimate future holds only encounter with death in one of its many forms. For when we try to understand our ethos from the point of view of responsiveness, we note that what we try to do in all our reactions to actions upon us is to make them fit into a large scheme of existence whose end is nothingness. Our actual ethics, personal and social, is to a large extent analyzable as defense ethics or as ethics of survival. It is the ethics of self-maintenance against threatening power that is not identifiable with any specific agency we meet but rather with a movement or a law in the interaction of all things, a law of our history. In our ethics of self-defense we act toward the realization of no ideal, unless continuing in existence is an ideal; we obey no law of reason, unless the law that reason itself must constantly defend itself and the body is a rational law. With our ethics of self-defense or survival we come to each particular occasion with the understanding that the world is full of enemies though it contains some friends. Hence we respond to all actions upon us with an evaluatory scheme: beings are either good or evil; they belong to the class of the things that ought to be or those that ought not to be. And ultimately the distinction between them has to be made by reference to the way they support or deny our life, whether this be our physical or spiritual or social existence. We can see fairly plainly how survival ethos works if we take society into view, which is in many ways, as Plato thought, the individual writ large.

Henri Bergson in his book *The Two Sources of Morality and Religion* has described in detail the defensive ethics of society, threatened by the corrosive action of rational criticism and the rebellion of the young. But we have many illustrations in contemporary history of defensive social ethics. In the destructive interactions of castes or racial groups in the United States and in South Africa and elsewhere in the world we must take into account that beyond all loyalty to law and beyond all idealism there is operative in the minds of the defensive group a deep fear of coming destruction. The future holds for it no promise, no great opportunities, but only loss and descent, if not into the grave then *ad inferos*. Its actions are those that seem to it to be fitting, i.e., to fit into a situation and into a history whose past is full of guilt, acknowledged or not, and whose future is full of death in one of its forms. How the ethics of survival or of defensiveness dominates international relations needs hardly to be pointed out. There it changes all our obediences, as when defensive democrats abandon their law of equality because they must defend themselves against those who have another law. It affects even religious groups from the Pharisees of the New Testament to those Protestants or Catholics who fear that God may die if they do not survive. As for defensiveness in personal ethos, common observation as well as psychological analysis bring to our attention how much our actions are those of men who try to do what they think is fitting, in order that they may maintain status in a society which they believe threatens them with isolated existence, with a kind of social death; or who must gather wealth or prestige or righteousness in order that they may be remembered, be not relegated to the realm of those who might as well not have been or otherwise end in nothingness.

In a time-full, historical life, moving from nothingness to nothingness, our ideals and laws all seem to give way before the demand to do what we think is fitting in such a situation. Or otherwise such ideals and laws are modified so that they may fit into this movement. Deontological thought tends to regard death and failure as the consequences of disobedience to the law. In the light of response analysis we are more inclined to regard death and its rule over our history as the source both of the law, at least of much of it, and of our multiplied transgressions. It is this rule of death that leads us to develop our defensive measures of *Thou shalt not*s and that isolates us from each other, individual by individual, group by group, each with the motto, "Self-preservation is the first law of life." Idealism and respect for the law of reason may protest, but man continues to do what seems to him fitting in such a history of guilt and fear of loss of himself.

V

IF THIS description of our human situation is at all correct, what has become of the decisive present, of freedom in the now? The responsive and responsible self is not a machine to be sure, but is it not ruled by tradition and memory on the one hand and on the other by an inescapable conviction about the death-dealing character of that total environment in which it does its fitting actions? We make our confident predictions about others' actions, individual or social, by means of this understanding of interpretation and response. We predict that they will act in self-defense—more or less enlightened; and our prophecy is usually correct. We expect that the Thou's and It's will act as they have done in the past—and usually do. We expect them to change their acknowledged laws and ideals when adherence to them would not lead to action that fits into such a history. And as a rule our expectations are verified.

Yet something like that freedom of which teleological and deontological thinkers speak in their different ways also comes into appearance when we analyze ourselves as responsive, time-full beings. The question of freedom arises in this connection as the question of the self's ability in its present to change its past and future and to achieve or receive a new understanding of its ultimate historical context. If these two modifications are possible, then reinterpretation of present action upon the self must result, and a new kind of reaction, a response that fits into another lifetime and another history, can and will take place.

There are at least two ways in which selves undertake to change their inherited patterns of interpreting the beings and actions to whom they respond in the present. One is the way of antitraditionalism; it is the way both of Descartes and of radical empiricism. It begins with radical doubt, undertaking to question every received notion and to form in the present moment new patterns for interpreting events. The method has had its great successes in the sphere of man's encounters with natural events. There he has learned to interpret the morning appearance of the sun and the moon's eclipse, the thunder and the lightning of the storm, changes of seasons and weather, the blowing of the wind, the birth of animals, the coming of illness to the body, the flowing of the blood, and a thousand other phenomena with the aid of new ideas. He has done this by resolutely putting aside, determinedly forgetting, his old anthropomorphic patterns of interpretations. Hence he responds to these meetings with fresh interpretations and with other reactions than those that have been inscribed into his social memory, that is, mostly into his ordinary language. What he calls his conquest of nature is for the most part less an assertion of dominance than a new interpreting of nature's ways, an interpreting of its special occasions as signs of larger and constant meanings; and then it is response to these occasions in accordance with the new interpretation. He has found the new responses more fitting. He is neither obedient nor disobedient to nature's laws, neither opposed to, nor associated with, its purposes. He simply undertakes to do the fitting thing—to carry out that action which will fit into natural action in view of all his future meetings with the natural forces. And at his best he has in view not only the way the action fits into his own life process but also into the whole natural process.

But this method of freeing ourselves from our past by putting it behind us has been notably successful only in our encounters with nature, and in the internal realm of our conscious reasoning about nature. Where we have tried to apply it to our responses to persons and to communities, it has been successful only to the extent to which we have been able to reduce selves to objects, to unknowing knowns, noninterpreting reactors. Despite the ancient and long cry that ethics must become scientific, after the fashion of the natural sciences, little seems to have been accomplished in the sphere of interpersonal action by means of the method of doubt and forgetting the past and making a fresh beginning.

There is, however, another way of changing the patterns of interpretation—a method more fitting to beings that have in every present an internal, remembered past which they cannot forget or leave behind. It is the way of *reinterpreting* the past. It recalls, accepts, understands, and reorganizes the past instead of abandoning it. As social persons living in the present with a social past we pursue this way through the study of our social history. It is notorious and yet deeply significant that every age tends to study again in the light of its new present the past it has brought along with it. In America we re-examine, generation after generation, our great national tragedy, the Civil War. Our ever-renewed attention to it has been in part, of course, simply an effort to maintain established patterns of interpretation so that in the present North and South, Negroes and whites, industrialists and agrarians, may encounter and respond to each other as they have always done. But to a large extent our study of that history has been a reconstruction of a past which is still in us, in conscious and unconscious ideas, and in complex associations of emotions with those ideas. Insofar as the reinterpretation of our past has led us to some new understanding and acceptance of the past actions of and upon our groups, our present encounters with each other as North and South, Negro and white, have been guided by somewhat new ideas. Every nation with similar social recollections of past animosities, with a similar inherited complex of emotional and personal attitudes of group to group, seeks, I believe, to move toward freedom, toward freshness and fittingness in present interaction by similar reconstructions of its past. International interactions doubtless require and in part receive the same kind of reinterpretation of past encounters; and so do the actions and reactions of religious groups upon each other. The constantly renewed study of the origins of Christianity means more for Christians than an effort to discover what is their purpose or their real law. It presents to them the questions (though they will not always acknowledge it): "How can they become free from being dominated by inherited images?" "How can they respond in the present not only to their fellow men, Jews and Romans—or the chosen people and the world—but to Jesus Christ, and to God, with reconstructed interpretations instead of with merely customary symbols and emotions?" So it is also with the study of the Reformation by Protestants and Catholics, the study of their origins by Methodists and Presbyterians, Anglicans and Baptists. We may of course study our histories in order to establish our defense mechanisms better. But we study them for the sake of reinterpretation.

More striking though perhaps not more important than the method of history is that method of reconstructing our personal past which men have begun to practice systematically under the leadership of analytical psychology. How deeply our unconscious as well as conscious memory affects our reactions to other persons in our present; what images of ourselves we carry with us as a result of past encounters reaching back to the day of birth; how the feelings of dependence, love, and aggression, attached to those past meetings, modify our interpretations of ourselves and others in the present—all this and much more has been brought to our attention by these psychologists. They have found that if present relations of selves to others are to be reorganized, if the responses of selves to others and to themselves in interaction with others, are to be made constructive rather than destructive, if they are to fit better into the total process of interpersonal life, then the past must not be forgotten but remembered, accepted, and reinterpreted. What such analysis calls again to our attention is related—though the exact character of the relation remains largely unclarified—to that understanding of themselves which Christians have had when they looked for newness of life not by way of forgetting the past but by the forgiveness of sin, the remembrance of their guilt, and the acceptance of their acceptance by those against whom they had offended. In the life of the self, responding to action upon it in the present, freedom from the past or newness of understanding and movement toward more fitting response does not come through the rejection of the past but through its reinterpretation. In the curious existence of the I, as a being living in three tenses, the reconstruction of our past can be a large part of our hope for the future.

The reinterpretation of the actions of others upon us—even of the action of our total environment upon us—which gives us the possibility of new response in the present, results also from reinterpretation of our future, since we react in the present predictively as well as in recollection. And as there are constancies and stereotypes in our recollections so also there are constancies in our predictions. Our actions in response to the actions upon us of natural powers are guided by the confidence with which we expect them to act in the future as we understood them to behave in the past. We react to the coming of spring with deeds anticipatory of summer and autumn and winter. We do the fitting thing less under the rule of law or of ideals than in expectancy of other actions than our own that will bring our seed to harvest. We administer our energies and resources in response to demands made upon us by our bodies in their interaction with their environments in anticipation always of future demands and of future certainties of physical decline and death. But we can revise, also, these predictions of the way that natural forces will behave in the future. We change our anticipations of the food supply that is to be available to us, or of the growth of human population, and in the light of such revisions change our reactions to present demands. We attempt to do what is fitting in anticipation of future scarcity or abundance. We reinterpret our future also as we identify ourselves with different groups. The industrialist who has been guiding his activities with a view to predicted events in the interactions of his enterprise with society becomes a government official; at once the future lengthens at the same time that the society broadens, and he begins to think responsively and responsibly in terms of generations rather than of a decade or at best two and in terms also of the interaction of his larger society with other nations. So also the statesman, revising his predictions of the future relations of presently inimical and friendly powers, responds to their present actions with new interpretations. What he previously thought fitting now seems no longer fitting because the pattern of anticipated future interaction has changed.

If we look in all this for the arbitrary free will, we can locate it only at the point where the agent commits himself to inquiry into the further, longer series of interactions and into the responses taking place in a larger society, or at the point where he commits himself to resolute questioning of the adequacy of his stereotyped, established interpretations.

VI

YET ALL of these social and personal reinterpretations of remembered pasts and anticipated futures do not radically change either our general pattern of understanding of action upon us or our general mode of fitting response so long as our sense of the ultimate context remains unrevised. Deep in our minds is the myth, the interpretative pattern of the metahistory, within which all our histories and biographies are enacted. It has variant forms. It appears as the story of recurring cycles, of golden, silver, bronze, and iron ages, or of the round of personal rebirth and death. It appears as the story of the infinite progress of a particular species, this human kind, moving outward into space with its conquests, forward in time with victories over nature, but leaving behind in its past forgotten, dead generations. And that is the great overarching myth. It is the almost unconquerable picture in the mind, of everlasting winter lying on the frozen wastes of existence before all its time and after all its time, or, otherwise, of all-destroying fire raging before and after the brief interval of its life upon our planet or in our galaxy. It is the image of myself as coming to that future when there is no more future. It is that understanding of the society, into whose actions I fit my actions, as bound with all the tragic empires of history toward the eschaton, beyond which there is no healing of diseases, no resurrection. It has scores of forms, no doubt, this mythology of death. But all its forms lead to the same interpretations in the present; to the same way of evaluating the beings with whom we are compresent by dividing them into the good and evil.

And all the forms lead to the ethos of defense, to the ethics of survival.

The great religions in general, and Christianity in particular, make their not least significant attack on this universal human ethos by challenging our ultimate historical myth. They do present new laws; they do present to us new ideals. But beyond all this they make their impact on us by calling into question our whole conception of what is fitting—that is, of what really fits in—by questioning our picture of the context into which we now fit our actions. Doubtless they develop certain accommodations in their popular forms to the mythology of death—as in those Christian teachings about heaven and hell that lead to a new Manichaeanism and to a new form of survival ethics. Doubtless they must also clothe in symbols and in legends the conviction that we are surrounded in history by life and not by death, by the power of being and not by ultimate destructiveness. These, like all human words and pictures, will be subject to misinterpretation, as when our existence in responsibility is all concentrated in the vision of a last judgment where the rule of law is thought to prevail. But despite all aberrations and deviations, the central work of revising our mythology of death into a history of life goes on and with it the redefining for us of what is fitting response in a lifetime and a history surrounded by eternal life, as well as by the universal society of being.

4

RESPONSIBILITY IN ABSOLUTE DEPENDENCE

IN THE preceding lectures I have attempted to develop my understanding of some aspects of our existence as selves, living in response to actions upon us in society and in time. Response to other selves and to things—to Thou's and It's—is, as it were, one dimension of our activity; response in that time-fullness in which our past and our future give depth and height to the present is another dimension. The fitting act is made to fit into a situation that is defined by more than one measurement, somewhat as the cabinet-maker takes many measurements of many surfaces and planes into account as he fits tenon into mortise. The parable, of course, is misleading insofar as it brings to mind the idea of man-the-maker; in his responsibility man has no such nicely fixed structures into which to insert his deeds. A more apt comparison is that of the motor-car driver who must make forty decisions each minute. Neither obedience to rules of the road, nor desire to arrive at his goal, offers sufficient basis for his conduct. We have noted also that as we respond in society to action upon us we interpret each immediate deed by referring to its context in the enlarging society in which it takes place. Our interpretation of the immediate depends on our sense of the ultimate community of interaction. So also the timefulness of our agency and of our historical interpretations are conditioned by our understanding of what lies at the limits of our time. In both cases something that we may call the religious element in our responses has come into view, meaning by the word, religion, in this connection man's relation to what is ultimate for him—his ultimate society, his ultimate history.

This element is brought more radically to our attention when we consider a third feature of our existence as selves who act, react, and interact, always as interpreting agents. The self that knows itself in encounter with others, finds itself to be absolutely dependent in its existence, completely contingent, inexplicably present in its here-ness and now-ness.

I am, and I am I. That "I am," and "I am I" here, now, bring to my awareness a radical deed which I cannot identify with any of the specific actions that have constituted the elements of my body. Yet "I" am so intimately related to my body that the life of the body and my being seem almost inseparable, so that with the philosophers of life I am inclined to say: "I am alive, therefore I am." Neither can I identify the radical action by which *I am,* with any of the actions that have constituted this mind, which is so closely related to the self that with Descartes I want to say: "I think, therefore I am." Nor is the action by which *I am* identifiable with that series of actions by which those emotions have come into being, which make the external observer regard me as a complex of feelings, a system of emotions, a temperament, an attitude, and which make me tend to say: "I feel, therefore I am." In all these statements the "I" has been posited in the premise. My self-existence is not deduced from something that is more evidently the case than that *I am*. There is no way of moving from the impersonal statements that thinking is going on, or that living is in process, or that feeling occurs, to the conclusion that therefore *I* am. Only if I posit the self can I refer this thinking, living, feeling, to myself.

As knowledge grows it is possible to identify and to interpret to an increasing extent the agencies that have acted on the elements of the self's body; explanations are forthcoming why its stature, its skin color, its sex, its tendency toward certain illnesses, and other biological facts about it are as they are. With such interpretations more or less at hand it is possible for the self to respond to the actions that have given its body such-and-such characteristics with perhaps ever more fitting reactions. Its responses will be more fitting in view of its own movement toward a continuation in physical being, toward health-giving interaction with natural forces, and in view of the biological community in which it interacts with others. But none of these interpretations of biological events touches the fact that it is *I* who am in or with this body, that *I* have this body, that this is *my* body. And none of the responses I make to the actions that constitute elements in my body are responses to the radical action by which *I am*.

As my understanding of actions upon me grows, I begin to identify the agencies by which thoughts have entered into my mind or the actions upon me to which I have responded as a thinking being, and so have come to have certain ideas and ways of thinking. I no longer tend to react to the ideas that are in my mind, for instance to these ideas of teleology and deontology or of fittingness in ethics, as though they were innate ideas or ideas of pure reason. I interpret the actions on my mind by which these ideas have come to me as historical actions in society; hence I respond with critical acceptance, correction, or rejection and try to think fitting thoughts in a living, changing social tradition of interaction among minds and of interaction between minds and objects. But none of these interpretations of the actions by which the ideas in my mind have come into being and are being modified, interprets for me this given fact, that it is I who am thinking in this here and now. Why a mind in the twentieth century should try to think about ethics with the aid of ideas of response—that, given the fact that it is interacting with other minds in this particular time in history, is explicable. What is not explicable to me by these means is that it is I who am now, inseparably connected with that mind; that I am in this moment with its past and future and not in the sixteenth or the eighth or the twenty-second century of the Christian era of this history of selves forming ideas, not to speak of being in China in the Ming dynasty or an Inca in Peru; that it is with this mind and these ideas that I must struggle. Nor is that response of mine to the questions and assertions of others in which I "make up my mind," a reply to that action by which I am and am in or with or through this mind.

What is to be said of ideas in general applies, of course, to my religious ideas, to my theology, to the ideas that have come to me in the midst of interaction with thinkers and speakers and writers in the Christian era, in Christendom, in the Christian church, or in Judaism, or in some other historic community of religious thinkers and believers. Because I can interpret the deeds through which my religious thoughts and practices have come to me—through parents, society, church, the general culture; because I can recall and reinterpret at least some of the emotional and intellectual responses I have made to these actions on me by finite agents, therefore I can respond to the continuing action upon me of religious men and institutions in more fitting ways than was possible before I understood such actions. My responses can be more fitting in the sense that they fit into the whole intellectual, emotional, religious process of my life more consistently and fit perhaps also more consistently and continuously into the action of my enlarging society. And yet after all this has been done two things remain uninterpreted: the radical action by which I was cast into this particular historical religious process, so that my interpretations and responses are directed toward particular challenges—in my case the challenges of the Christian religion; and the action by which I am. The category of fate, as Karl Heim called it, comes to my attention in the fact that I have no way of beginning religiously outside of my history, in abstraction from my society. Jesus Christ is my fate in Heim's words, whether I accept or reject him. If I respond to the giveness of my historic religion with the answer of atheism, I shall still be a Christian atheist. My denial will be dependent on the affirmation that I deny. As Christian atheist I shall be a different sort of denier and affirmer than a pre-Christian atheist was. My very reasons for atheism will be different. If this is true in my critically denying responses, it is evidently truer in my critically affirmative answers to religious acts of my society upon me. There is no way of being a religious self as such, any more than there is a way of being a thinking or a feeling or a speaking self as such. I am fated to be these things in the thus-ness and so-ness of my given historicity.

The radical action by which I am and by which I am present with this body, this mind, this emotional equipment, this religion, is not identifiable with any of the finite actions that constitute the particular elements in physical, mental, personal existence. In my social, ego-alter existence, I know that this intensely private experience of selfhood is not solipsistic. Communication about the experience may be difficult; yet it is less difficult than communication about many public events. My companions speak about their problem in ways that intelligibly correspond to the ways that I must speak about mine. From the child's question, "Why I am I?" to Heidegger and Jaspers and Marcel's probing of the mystery; from the agonized questioning of the bereaved mother, "Why did this happen to *me?*" to the statesman's wonder why he was matched with his peculiar hour and his particular nation; from Hamlet's distaste of his body's solid flesh back to ancient speculations about the soul's tomb, and forward toward modern efforts to help selves find their identity—I am surrounded by the questions of Thou's who are I's like me, and ask about the action that cast them into being, and into such a specific history among such other beings in the given-ness of society and time.

The radical nature of the action by which I am, in the thus-ness and so-ness of existence, its here-ness and now-ness, has astonished many a thinker besides the modern existentialist. One who is more frequently classified with the naturalists than with the existentialists, Professor Santayana, in a speech delivered at the celebration of the tercentenary of Spinoza's birth, spoke in this wise:

"In what I am about to say . . . I do not mean to prejudge any cosmological questions, such as that of free will or necessity, theism or pantheism. I am concerned only with the sincere confessions of a mind that has surrendered every doubtful claim and every questionable assurance. Of such assurances or claims there is one which is radical and comprehensive: I mean, the claim to existence and to directing the course of events. We say conventionally that the future is uncertain: but if we withdrew honestly into ourselves and examined our actual moral resources, we should feel that what is insecure is not merely the course of particular events but the vital presumption that there is a future coming at all, and a future pleasantly continuing our habitual experience. We rely in this, as we must, on the analogies of experience, or rather on the clockwork of instinct and presumption in our bodies; but existence is a miracle, and morally considered, a free gift from moment to moment. That it will always be analogous to itself is the very question we are begging. Evidently all interconnections and sequences of events, and in particular any consequences which we may expect to flow from our actions, are really entirely beyond our spiritual control. When our will commands and seems, we know not how, to be obeyed by our bodies and by the world, we are like Joshua seeing the sun stand still at his bidding; when we command and nothing happens, we are like King Canute surprised that the rising tide should not obey him; and when we say we have executed a great work and re-directed the course of history, we are like Chanticleer attributing the sunrise to his crowing.

"What is the result? That at once, by a mere act of self-examination and frankness, the spirit has come upon one of the most important and radical of religious perceptions. It has perceived that though it is living, it is powerless to live; that though it may die, it is powerless to die; and that altogether, at every instant and in every particular, it is in the hands of some alien and inscrutable power."[1]

The long quotation calls our attention to some specific features of the radical action by which the self is, and is thus and so, among the equally contingent beings and processes which in its animal faith it takes for granted. The action by which I am, is not one by which I was thrown into existence at some past time to maintain myself thereafter by my own power. It is the action whereby I am now, so that it seems truer to say that I am being lived than that I live. I live but do not have the power to live. And further, I may die at any moment but I am powerless to die. It was not in my power, nor in my parents' power, to elect my *self* into existence. Though they willed a child or consented to it they did not will *me* —this I, thus and so. And so also I now, though I *will* to be no more, cannot elect myself out of existence, if the inscrutable power by which I am, elects otherwise. Though I wish to be mortal, if the power that threw me into being in this mortal destructible body elects me into being again there is nothing I can do about that. I can destroy the life of my body. Can I destroy myself? This remains the haunting question of the literature of suicide and of all the lonely debates of men to whom existence is a burden. Whether they shall wake up again, either here in this life or there

---

[1] George Santayana, "Ultimate Religion," *Obiter Scripta,* ed. J. Buchler and B. Schwartz (New York: Charles Scribner's Sons, 1936), pp. 283 f.

in some other mode of being, is beyond their control. We can choose among many alternatives; but the power to choose self-existence or self-extinction is not ours. Men can practice birth-control, not self-creation; they can commit *bio*cide; whether they can commit suicide, self-destruction, remains a question.

II

THE RADICAL action whereby we are ourselves in the here and now, as thus and so, cannot be classified in that series of actions of finite powers to which we respond in accordance with our more or less enlightened interpretations. We can interpret the questions addressed to us by companions. We can understand the meaning of the action in which a companion wounds our bodies or our feelings. We can ask what this action means in its larger context (not only what he consciously means by it), and so interpreting we can make a more fitting reply. But how is the self to interpret the radical action that flings it into existence and holds it there? It cannot refer back to events in which something similar happened to it; it cannot use analogies, saying that this action is something like another action it has experienced before. The experience is unique, though it is repeated by millions of selves.

Because of the uniqueness of the radical act by which I am— the act, let us say, of fate; because there seems to be nothing that I can do about it; because it is painful to think of the absolute dependence in which I have been established; or for a score of other reasons, my usual reaction to that act is to try to forget it; to be unresponsive to it; and so to move in unresponsiveness and irresponsibility so far as this central self is concerned. This is to accept the familiar pattern of self-ignoring existence to which the existentialists in modern times but many sociologists in their way also have called our attention. Though the strange question of the I came to the self in youth, though it encountered the alien power by which it existed—the mystery of being—it was soon distracted from attending to this daily, momentary, momentous action upon it and was directed by its companions to concentrate on less radical encounters, particularly on encounters with the generalized other of society itself. It was taught to substitute for the question, "What am I?" the general question, "What is man?" or, "What is a rational creature?" or, "What is a Christian?" or, "What is a Briton or an American?" It was led to ask practically, not "What must I do?" but "What is it fitting for man to do vis-à-vis that nature which has brought forth the human species along with other animal species?" or "What is the fitting thing one ought to do as a Christian? or as a member of Western culture? as an organization man?" For the word "I" we substitute now the word "one"; the "I" now becomes one among many, yet not one self among many selves; it is just one living body among many bodies; one thinking mind among many minds; one complex of feelings among many such complexes. So the person loses himself in a mass and responds not as a self but as a part of a machine, or of a field of forces, or of a system of ideas. It responds in all its action not to the act by which it is a self but to the action by which the group of bodies or of minds or of emotions exists. The self does not exist in the presence of its maker or of the action that makes it; a mind exists in the presence of its objects; a body exists vis-à-vis natural forces; a conscience exists in encounter with society. Some social psychologists call this situation one in which the self is "Other-directed" rather than "self-directed"; we might call it the situation of response to all others except that otherness by which the self is self, and of response therefore by forces in the body and the mind, but not by the self as self. Heidegger speaks of it as the state of our lostness, *Verlorenheit,* where the self is lost among objects and is itself a kind of object; we might speak of it as the state of our unresponsiveness as *selves.* In this state we say "I think" but really mean "It seems"; we say "I believe" but really mean "It appears likely." Even contracts, promises, and commitments are made in a third-person mood as though our signature on the bond meant "Someone will see to it that this one or its heirs will meet this obligation." We may even make the commitment "I will love, honor, and keep thee" as though it meant "It seems likely something in me will continue to love, respect, and be good to you."

There is a more thoughtful way of interpreting and responding to the radical action whereby the I is thrown into existence. This is the way of the East primarily, though it has some counterparts in Western wisdom. Instead of ignoring the radical action whereby I am I, such wisdom attends to it and interprets it as the action of a deluding power. "There is no sorrow like existence: no bliss greater than Nirvana."[2] "It is desire, it is wrath, that is the voracious one, the wicked. Know thou that in this world there is the great enemy, as a flame hidden in a cloud of smoke . . . so is this world enveloped by desire."[3] And desire is chiefly the desire to be a self. Self-consciousness, to use our Western language, is the great illusion whence arise the sorrows and the cruelties of existence, or it is the demonic power in men that must be exorcised by discipline and contemplation until complete self-renunciation is achieved. It is not by losing oneself in the common mind of the mass that proper response is made to the power by which the self exists. To do this is not to take seriously enough the radical character of the action by which the self comes into being, nor to understand how its response to that action qualifies all its other actions. For such wisdom the self encounters the great enemy in the power by which it is; the enemy must not be ignored but combated with wise strategy.

To one who in his personal history has had to deal with the radical action whereby he is with the aid of his Christian companions' interpretations, it seems clear that both these ways—that of ignor-

---

[2] Dhammapada; cf. K. Saunders, *The Ideals of East and West* (New York: The Macmillan Company, 1934), p. 28.

[3] From the Gītā; cf. Saunders, *op. cit.*, p. 35.

ing the action and that of interpreting it as inimical—are primarily expressions of faith, but it is faith in its negative form of distrust. When we say that the interpretation of the radical action is made in faith, we use the word, faith, not as meaning some set of beliefs that must take the place of knowledge until knowledge is possible. The aspect of faith we have here in mind is simply that trust or distrust which is said by some psychologists to be the basic element in the development of personality in a child's first year and to which theologians, notably Luther, have pointed as the fundamental element in religion. Faith is the attitude of the self in its existence toward all the existences that surround it, as beings to be relied upon or to be suspected. It is the attitude that appears in all the wariness and confidence of life as it moves about among the living. It is fundamentally trust or distrust in being itself. Such faith is an ingredient in all knowing, as the reliance present in such knowing on the constancy of the processes observed in nature and as reliance also on the fellow men who report their observations. It is present in its negative form of distrust in all the inquiries we make about the group actions of our national or religious friends and allies. Such faith is never the antithesis of knowledge but its accompaniment; though in some instances there is preponderance of faith over knowledge, and in others preponderance of knowledge over faith, as may be evident in the form of a statement. "I believe you" is a statement of faith though it contains an element of knowledge or acknowledgment. "Many of you are members of Glasgow University" is a statement of fact, but is said with some confidence in what I have been told and seen.

Faith as trust or distrust accompanies all our encounters with others and qualifies all our responses. But it is the chief ingredient in our interpretation of the radical act or agency by which we are selves, here and now. To be sure, some element of that other species of faith—the great hypotheses about the what and how of our becoming and of the becoming of all things—may accompany our trust interpretation. Theories of creation, of how the contingent world came into being, whether in six days five thousand years ago, or in aeons six billion years ago, whether by design or by accident, whether by artistry or by growth—these may accompany our interpretation of the act whereby we are and are in our world. But such ardently or lightly held hypotheses express rather than found the fundamental faith interpretation in its trust or distrust of the alien and inscrutable power that elects us and all things into existence. We seem to differ in our response to that power, not because in religious or secular thinking we hold variant theories of the origin of existent reality, but because we interpret in trust or in distrust the act by which we ourselves are and are in this world.

When we say that the power by which we are is God, we may express our interpretation in trust, for to say "God" is to say "good" in our common speech; the word, God, means the affirmer of our being, not its denier; "God" means the concern of the ultimate for what issues from it, not its heedlessness or its animosity. Yet it is quite possible to say that the power is "God" and still express distrust, since the word, God, may mean for us a power that is jealous of its rights, that is suspicious of its creation, that is as ready to deny it, to condemn it to destruction and to damn it to everlasting grief, as to affirm, maintain, and bless it. The question of our fundamental interpretation is not to be settled therefore by asking what words we use, any more than it can be answered by asking about the theories of creation that we employ. Our primordial interpretation of the radical action by which we are is made in faith as trust or distrust. Between these two there seems to be no middle term. The inscrutable power by which we are is either for us or against us. If it is neutral, heedless of the affirmations or denials of the creatures by each other, it is against us, to be distrusted as profoundly as if it were actively inimical. For then it has cast us into being as aliens, as beings that do not fit.

Trust or distrust of being or, better, of the power by which I am and we are, is a highly personal response. Of course it has its social aspects. The trust of my companions in the power by which they are, and also their loyalty to me and to our common causes, does influence my trust or distrust in the ultimate. But it remains questionable whether the self is led more to trust in the ultimate because it finds all the finite beings about it unreliable, or more because it is led by stages from trust in the near-at-hand to trust in the ultimate. Is it because all finite powers on which we have relied for value have failed us that we turn to the ultimate? or because we have seen traces of the structure of faith in the whole realm of being that we are led to confidence in Being simply considered? Trust and distrust in the ultimate power of being affect and are affected by all the interactions of trust and suspicion among the Thou's and It's. Yet the immediacy of the self's relation to the power by which it is cannot be supplanted by the mediation of any group of believers. Theology and doctrine are always highly social, representing our responses to each other's reports and interpretations of encounter with the ultimate. But faith as trust and distrust is inexpugnably personal. Of the theories I hold about God and man and human history I may say that they constitute "no faith of my own" but that of the church. But trust and distrust are my very own. In this faith, by this faith, I live. The ways in which I shall formulate and justify and express my trust or distrust in words or ritual acts are largely dependent on the social and historical setting in which I make my double response to the radical act and to all the finite actions, but what is formulated and expressed in such words is individual and personal. I do not respond, I am not responsible, to the ultimate power if I lapse into the responses of the group, respond as one who among other things is also a Christian or Jew or agnostic. In the realm of social religion no less than elsewhere the disappearance of the self in a mass, the escape from personal response and responsibility, is an ever-present possibility. Indeed social religion may provide particular temptations for escape from such responsibility, as educational institutions may provide particular temptations to evade the challenge of knowing for myself. Kierkegaard's attack on mass Christianity was doubtless made with a somewhat inadequate interpretation of social institutions in mind. It was not quite fitting, but the truth that is in it was not overstated. "When everyone is a Christian, no one is a Christian." The faith that is not my own but a unit of a mass is not trust or loyalty. It may be a content of a common mind.

The response in trust or distrust to the radical act of the self's and its world's creation qualifies all particular interpretations of finite actions upon the self and therefore all its reactions. There is, to be sure, also such a thing as a peculiarly or primarily religious response. We find this in the almost spontaneous acts of praise or gratitude for our being and for the world around us, or in the antithetical actions of rejection, of cursing the power that brought us forth and made such men in such a world. There are also the direct faith responses of commitment, whether these be in the form of resolutions of reliance ("Father, into thy hands I commit my spirit" or "Though he slay me yet will I trust him") or of loyalty. But for the most part the response of faith to the radical action by which the self is, is present as a qualifying element in all interpretations and reactions to the movements of that finite world of particular beings in which the I is involved.

How this is the case can be clarified, I believe, if we try to answer some questions about our interpretations (and reactions) to what is going on about us in the daily round of events. One of these is the question: "How is it possible to be *one* self in the multiplicity of events and of one's interpretations of them? How does the self as such become responsible instead of remaining a concatenation of responsive systems, fitting their actions now into this, now into that series of events?" The sociologists who speak of the many roles a person plays in his relation to different groups do not seem to answer the question about the one self that is pres-

ent in all the roles. The psychologists who speak of self-identifica-
tion as a process of self-distinction from the dominant others do not
adequately tell me with what it is that the distinct self identifies itself. Some systems of unity are achieved within the self when it
interprets particular events as instances of general behavior, dis-
cerns natural constancies at work in natural occasions and social
constancies in the behavior of companion individuals in their various aggregates. Man responsive and responsible before nature, fitting his actions into those of nature; man responsive in political or
economic or cultural society as responsible citizen; responsible
businessman, responsible educator, responsible scientist, responsible parent, responsible churchman—such men we know and understand. But what ties all these responsivities and responsibilities
together and where is the responsible *self* among all these roles
played by the individual being? Can it be located within the self,
as though by some mighty act of self-making it brought itself into
being as one "I" among these many systems of interpretation and
response? The self as one self among all the systematized reactions
in which it engages seems to be the counterpart of a unity that lies
beyond, yet expresses itself in, all the manifold systems of actions
upon it. In religious language, the soul and God belong together;
or otherwise stated, I am one within myself as I encounter the One
in all that acts upon me. When my world is divided into two
domains, the natural and the supernatural, or the physical and
the spiritual, or the secular and the religious, in which different
powers are interpreted as at work, and different meanings and
patterns of actions are evident, then I have two selves. But insofar
as in (faith) trust I acknowledge that whatever acts upon me, in
whatever domain of being, is part of, or participates in, one ultimate action, then though I understand nothing else about the
ultimate action, yet I am now one. Or, to state the matter in another way, by that action whereby I am I in all the roles I play, in
reaction to all the systems of action that impinge upon me, I am in

the presence of the One beyond all the many. And my response to every particular action takes the form of response also to the One that is active in it. I react to the actions of nature with the question, "What general truth is expressed in them?" but also with the query, "What universal truthfulness is here; and, what does this whole system of nature mean in its relation to these other systems of action—for instance, our human thinking itself and our human existence?" To respond to the ultimate action in all responses to finite actions means to seek one integrity of self amidst all the integrities of scientific, political, economic, educational, and other cultural activities; it means to be one responding self amidst all the responses of the roles being played, because there is present to the self the One other beyond all the finite systems of nature and society.

How response to the radical action whereby I am I, and things are as they are, qualifies all particular reactions is also clarified, I think, when—turning back to the subjects of our second and third lectures—we ask: "In what society and in what time do we make our responses to immediate actions upon us?" or "In what society and in what time do we interpret them as taking place?" I place every action in some society or company of interaction and in some history. The act is understood only because its relations are understood, and the question is about the extent of its relations, about its context. Is my reaction to my opponent guided by my locating him in the small society of which I am the center so that he is my enemy, or in the larger society of those who serve the same cause—be it the life of knowledge or political life or cultural life —so that he appears as the critic of my ideas or proposals; or do I see him in universal society, so that he appears in all his animosity and all his criticism as my fellow servant? When I respond to the One creative power, I place my companions, human and subhuman and superhuman, in the one universal society which has its center neither in me nor in any finite cause but in the Transcendent One. And the response is accordingly qualified. And so it is with the historical location of the action to which I answer. In what time do I see it? in my time? in my culture's or religion's time? or *sub specie aeternitatis*—in time inclusive of all times?

Finally there is the question of the evaluation that is present in all my interpretations. The actions to which I answer are valued as important or unimportant; they are good or bad, right or wrong. But for what and for whom are they important and unimportant, good or bad? In making my interpretations I abstract from the general situation and try to understand the importance or unimportance of some being presented to me or some event happening in my presence by reference to some hypothetical center. I may only ask: "Is this food good for my stomach?" "Is that line of thought important for the clarification of my thesis?" "Is the passing of this or that law conducive to the peace of my community?" So I move among many relative systems of good and evil and make many specific responses in accordance with these evaluating interpretations. But all these technical responses are imbedded, as it were, in larger systems of evaluation. The sentences in which I state my value-judgments are parts of paragraphs, the paragraphs of chapters, the chapters of a book. And the book is less the consequence of adding sentence to sentence, than the sentences are functions of the book, made to fit into the book. All my specific and relative evaluations expressed in my interpretations and responses are shaped, guided, and formed by the understanding of good and evil I have *upon the whole*. In distrust of the radical action by which I am, by which my society is, by which this world is, I must find my center of valuation in myself, or in my nation, or in my church, or in my science, or in humanity, or in life. Good and evil in this view mean what is good for me and bad for me; or good and evil for my nation, or good and evil for one of these other finite causes, such as mankind, or life, or reason. But should it happen that confidence is given to me in the power by which all things are and by which I am; should I learn in the depths of my existence to praise the creative source, than I shall understand and see that, *whatever is, is good,* affirmed by the power of being, supported by it, intended to be, good in relation to the ultimate center, no matter how unrighteous it is in relation to finite companions. And now all my relative evaluations will be subjected to the continuing and great correction. They will be made to fit into a total process producing good—not what is good for me (though my confidence accepts that as included), nor what is good for man (though that is also included), nor what is good for the development of life (though that also belongs in the picture), but what is good for being, for universal being, or for God, center and source of all existence.

Thus the responsible self finds its unity in its explicit responsiveness to the deed by which it is a self, one *I* among all its roles, and in its responsiveness to one action in all the actions to which it is subjected. The moral problem of the *one in the many* on its subjective side is the problem of the one self given to the I and required of it in all the pluralism of its being. That oneness, that "I am I," is given. It represents an action issuing in the self and maintaining the self. To respond to it is to respond to *my* maker. No matter how responsible I may be in my various roles as member of societies and holder of offices, I am not a whole, responsible self until I have faced up to this action, interpreted it, and given my answer.

On its objective side the moral problem of the one in the many is the problem of discerning one action, one intention, one final context of all the actions upon me, whether these issue from natural powers or from men, from It's or Thou's. The self which is one in itself responds to all actions upon it as expressive of One intention or One context. For it there is no evil in the city but the Lord has done it; no crucifixion but the One has crucified. How and why these events fit in, it does not yet know. So far as it acknowledges in positive or negative faith, in trust or in distrust, the One in the many, it accepts the presence only of One action in all actions upon it.

These two unities are inseparable from each other. I am one in my many-ness in myself and so responsible as self, as I face the One action in the actions of the many upon me.

Monotheistic idealism says: "Remember God's plan for your life." Monistic deontology commands: "Obey God's law in all your obediences to finite rules." Responsibility affirms: "God is acting in all actions upon you. So respond to all actions upon you as to respond to his action."

Our action in our lostness, however, is the action of distrust. We have our unity as selves it seems only as sinners who deeply distrust the One in all the many. Yet such distrust is occasionally converted into trust. On this subject of our responsibility in sin and salvation we must try to throw some light from the standpoint of response-analysis in the last lecture.

5

RESPONSIBILITY IN SIN AND SALVATION

THE FINAL question to which I address myself in this series of
lectures on a Christian philosophy of our human moral life is:
"Does the effort to view our self-action as responsive and responsible yield any insight into that complex of problems of self-
understanding to which we refer in the Christian community with
the aid of the words 'sin' and 'salvation' or 'redemption'?"

"Die Welt liegt im argen."[1] Christian thinkers have most com-
monly used the legal method in interpreting the human condition
of self-contradiction, of internal conflict in individual and society,
of alienation from self, neighbor, and the Transcendent that they
have seen prevalent among all men. Under the influence of Paul's
Letter to the Romans in particular, I believe we tend to read the
Scriptures and the story of our life with minds generally dominated

---

[1] I John 5:19 (Luther's translation).

by the symbol of man-under-law. So we think of the contradiction in which we are involved as one like that of the criminal who rebels against the social law while yet living under it and needing to have it maintained if his rebellious action is to have desired consequences. It is like the self-contradictoriness of lying, since the liar must desire that the law of truthtelling be generally observed if his transgression is to be helpful to him. Or this inner contradiction is like that of the man who recognizes two conflicting laws, a universal natural, right law, and a particular, provincial law, a law in the mind and a law in the members, the law of the realm of death and that of the realm of life, the law of a demonically ruled society and the law of God's kingdom. Or again the duality is like that of the anarchic rebel who asserts himself against the overarching realm of law and discovers that he must enact and obey new laws in the midst of his rebellion against all law in order to maintain himself and his rebellious community.

When we approach our human condition with this pattern predominantly in mind, we undertake to trace the source of our present evil condition to some transgression in our past. Not only the Christian does this; the tendency to regard man's present condition as miserable compared with some happy past or his potential state is so general that one is inclined to think that the idea of a fall is practically universal. Communism believes in a fall no less than does Christianity. Rousseau believes in it no less than does Augustine; Spinoza no less than Thomas. And every political party has its theory about how we got into the present mess. Almost universal also seems to be the thought that such a fall is connected with the giving or transgression of law. In our narrow societies we tend to place the blame for present wretchedness on some disobedience of our own in the past, or of our parents, or of the leaders of our nation, or of a larger society. There are those who identify the fall and the coming of wretchedness with the beginning of the First or the Second World War, or the rise of

Russia, or the industrial revolution, or the Reformation, or the Constantinian settlement, or the coming of civilization itself. They tend also to ascribe it to some willful defiance of a good law, thought to have been recognized and obeyed up to that time, or at least recognizable and obeyable. The Christian understanding of man—perhaps that of all radical monotheists—does not differ quite so much from other theories of the human condition because it posits a fall, but because it puts it at the origin of the history of human selves and so thinks of it as something in which all such selves and the whole self participate. Yet that is not our present point. This is rather that man's self-contradictory wretchedness is interpreted by Christians as well as by many others as primarily due to disobedience.

When this ruling symbol is used the consequences of sin are of course also interpreted with the aid of the same image, guilt within the self and punishment coming to it from without. The questions that arise are whether experienced and objective guilt are commensurable; whether the punishment fits the crime; why the innocent suffer and the unrighteous flourish. Much of the long debate that went on in the Old Testament community about the righteousness of God, and much of the following discussion in the New Testament community and between later Christians and their companions in the world, is carried on with this assumption accepted by all parties. Right life is obedient life, obedient to right rules; sin is transgression. The consequence of sin is or should be, therefore, the legal consequence, punishment, whether by punishment one means primarily the effort to right the balance in a society, or to maintain the law's majesty, or to attempt to reform the transgressor, or to warn others against committing like transgression, or all of these together. With the symbol of law and transgression firmly established, the development of ideas of universal law and of a universal judgment and of an eternal punishment or reward seem logically to follow, when the scene of our human action is understood as that of the universal society under law in infinite time.

What happens to the understanding of man's salvation from sin and its consequences, when the law-symbol predominates, is illustrated in the whole story of our Christian and also our generally human reflection on this theme. Salvation is the *justification* of the transgressor, his *acquittal* before the universal court despite his guilt. Its condition is repentance interpreted as acknowledgment of guilt and sorrow for sin and perhaps also the substitutionary punishment of another, the Christ. The life of the redeemed is conceived often as life under a new or higher law or, more adequately, as life lived in obedience to an inner law, inscribed upon the heart. The standard terms of theology all reflect the presence to the mind of legal imagery, justification by faith, substitutionary atonement, the righteousness of God, etc.

Very much highly illuminating thought about ourselves in sin and salvation has been developed in Christianity and Christendom with the aid of the legal symbol. With its aid also, and doubtless more significantly, the actual life of selves has been deeply modified. The symbols of commandment, obedience, justification, repentance for transgression, are so deeply imbedded in the language of Christian faith—particularly in the direct I-Thou discourse of prayer and confession—that it is difficult to understand how the actual experience of our existence in wretchedness and in glory, in bondage and in freedom, in death and in life, could be grasped and shaped without this imagery.

And yet it is notorious that paradoxes accumulate for us as we try to understand ourselves in society and time before God, with the use of this symbolism. There is the paradox of law and gospel, which is not only the subject of much theological debate but manifests itself in the dilemmas of a practical reasoning that seeks, for instance, to reconcile the requirement of the law to love God with heart, soul, mind, and strength and the neighbor as oneself, with the spontaneity, the unrequired character, of genuine love. To love in obedience to requirement is not to love at all; yet it is required that one love unrequiredly. There is the similar paradox in the reflection that the action of the redeemed must be obedient to the will of another than the self, namely, God, and yet that if redeemed it be done in freedom, namely, in the doing of one's own will. These and other dilemmas appear and reappear in the efforts of Christian moral theologians to set forth the reason in the Christian ethos, as when Karl Barth sets forth the law as a form of the gospel but in doing so turns the idea of demand (*Gebot*) into the idea of permission; or when a Bultmann, describing Jesus Christ's action as one of radical obedience, eliminates all specific reference to a law or a requirement to which the radically obedient man is obedient. Of the logical dilemmas encountered in theological theories of atonement that operate with the symbolism of laws and courts I will not speak at all.

Such linguistic and logical difficulties encountered in practical as well as in speculative reasoning do not, of course, mean that the deontological approach to the definition of ourselves in theory and practice is invalid; but they do raise the question of the adequacy of the grand hypothesis, namely, that our life as agents in sin and salvation is fundamentally that of men-under-law or of obedience. They raise the question whether we are not letting ourselves be ruled too much by a single great symbol which is something less than an image of the whole process with which we are concerned as time-full, social beings—sinful and saved before God.

With the use of the alternative symbol of man-the-maker or man-the-realizer of ideals, we understand our human wretchedness, self-contradictoriness, and alienation as *hamartia,* the missing of the mark, rather than as transgression of the law. Sin is not quite so much lawbreaking as vice; it is the perverse direction of the drives in man, or of his will in general, toward ends not proper to him. Though vice leads to transgression of the law, yet this transgression is not the basic evil in self-existence. The fundamental evil is conflict within, and corruption of, a life meant by its internal entelechy, its native drive, to be whole and ordered within itself, whether as personal, or as social or universal. For the individualistic idealist the disorder in man is the multiplicity of his loves, all tending toward separate ends, unordered in a complete life directed toward a single goal, unformed in accordance with a unifying image. Or it is the disorder that results when the self holds before itself an image of itself that is not in accordance with its actual constitution and when it thus moves against its own grain. For the social idealist the disorder in mankind is to be found in the contradictory ends striven after by various groups in what is yet one society. In this contradiction the individuals that are members of more than one group participate, as they play their various roles, with such contradictory images before them as those of the patriotic nationalist, the good European, the white man, the democrat, the successful economic man, the aesthetic man, the Christian, etc. For the universal teleologist, the Christian now particularly, all these contradictions in individual and society are recognizably present, but the fundamental disorder is traced to the fact that the self has set before itself an image to be realized in action which runs counter to its place as a creature. Man wants to be like God, not only in the knowledge of good and evil, but in being his own maker. The point for such an idealist is, of course, not that man should live under law rather than be a maker, but that when he seeks to make himself into conformity to any image except the one destined for him he involves himself in self-destruction as well as in the destruction of others. As is the case with the deontologist, the Christian idealist does not differ as a rule from others who employ the same symbolism, by reason of his belief that man is disordered or full of vice. On that point there is again general agreement. The difference is likely to be the same one we have noted among deontologists; the radically monotheistic thinker sees the human disorder as involving the whole career of the self in all time and in all human selfhood. Like his deonto-logical counterpart, the Christian teleologist understands the human condition of self-contradiction and wretchedness as having origi-nated with the very origin of self-existence as self-knowing and self-directing, whether he interprets the Genesis story of the first sin as history, saga, or myth. Yet the center of the fall story for him is subtly different from that of the deontologist. The tragic center of the tale lies in man's yielding to the temptation to aspire after godhead rather than in his disobedience to commandment.

If the symbol of man-the-maker is consistently employed, the consequence of the first sin is understood as loss and confusion, rather than as guilt. The high goal, the ultimate form of good, is lost to view and the ability to pursue it disappears from life with the removal of the great attractive goal. The possibility of seek-ing lower good ends remains, but with the departure from view of the inclusive, unifying ultimate end, confusion enters, as the desires active in man tend toward their separate ends. Salvation comes with the restoration of the vision of God to man, and the reflected image of God in him. It is less the establishment of inno-cence from transgression than the granting to the self of ability to move again toward perfection, toward the actualization of the power by which it is enabled to see God and to live in his likeness. Salvation is the restoration of the goal that had been lost and so also the healing of the diseased powers.

As in the case of deontology, the application of this scheme of self-interpretation yields many insights into our human nature in general and the Christian life in particular. It is also an effective guide to conduct for the individual and for the church as it under-takes its pastoral ministry of caring for men who have lost the image yet can be kept in some health in the midst of their weakness and illness and to whom the hope of eternal life, the vision of God and the image of God, are communicated through word and sacrament. But that the great scheme of interpretation is not adequate, that much in experience must be left out of account when human existence in general and Christian life in particular are so understood, seems to be evident from the two facts that the deontological theory must be maintained alongside the teleological, even by the teleologists themselves, and that there are paradoxes present in such teleological interpretation.

The paradoxes that appear in teleology differ from those that come into view for deontology. The problem of law and gospel is of no great import for those who see this life as aspiration toward the vision and the image of God. But the paradox of the *vision* and the *image* is acute for them. On the one hand the great goal of life is *God*—God seen, God known, God loved. On the other hand it is the *perfection* of the seer, the knower, the lover. Thomas Aquinas maintains that it does not make a significant difference whether we speak first of the perfection of the self or first of the objective reality toward which the perfect self is directed in its activity. But in practice it does make a great difference whether the end is defined as the subjective good or the objective, whether as residing in the self or in the not-self, whether as love or the loved object. The strictures developed by critics of all self-conscious pursuers of perfection, whether these be monks and nuns or Protestant third orders, are germane and important. So it does make a difference whether I seek to be a loving self or seek my neighbor; whether my goal is to be a good man, or whether it is a good that lies beyond me as my object, for instance, justice in my society; whether I want to be religious or want to see God. Practice and its consequences raise questions about the adequacy of the theory. Other paradoxes center around the themes of the range of divine and human action. The theory of teleology, whether Christian or non-Christian, always directs attention to the primacy of the *human* pursuit of the ideal good. But it remains most difficult to reconcile this with the Christian conviction and experience of the primacy of *God's* action: in making himself known by the revelation of his goodness rather than allowing himself to be found by search; in giving the faith, the love, and the hope that aspire toward him; in creating and re-creating, making and remaking. There is always a surd, a contradiction, when the image of man-the-maker and the image of God-the-creator and re-creator are combined in one picture.

In the efforts of Christians to understand their human nature in sin and salvation and so to give direction to their practice, the two modes of approach are usually combined. The law is introduced into the scheme of salvation by restoration of the image, or the idea of perfection is introduced into a scheme of thinking that takes obedience as its point of departure. Such a combination of theories is characteristic of common-sense thinking in the church. But the combination is never perfect. There is strife between the two views at many points. The continued argument in theology between the two schools of thought and practice, the charges of heresy or of misinterpretation of the Scriptures, of Pelagianism and legalism, of sacrificing the human to the divine, or vice versa, that the two dominant ways of approach make against each other; the differences in the practices of churchmanship, of preaching, of exercising pastoral care, of administering the sacraments, etc., that obtain between the two modes of self-existence in Christian faith —all these point to the inadequacy of either theory by itself to give unified insight into the complex experience of man's existence in sin and salvation. Each approach leads to paradox and the combination remains incomplete. Now it is the task of theology, of moral theology in this case, to uncover the source of confusions and paradoxes; it is its task to bring greater clarity to the self in its agency, not by supplying a theory on which practice may follow, but by illuminating the theory that is actually though unacknowledgedly present in practice.

II

WE SHALL make the attempt, therefore, to interpret our Christian human experience as agents, sinful yet saved, with the aid of response-analysis to see whether this theory enables us to avoid the difficulties of teleology and deontology while yet making room for the insights these methods have yielded. The paradoxes of deontology, centering in the problems of law and gospel, are solvable, it seems to me, if we note that obedience to commandment is indeed response to one kind of action upon us, but that our response is to other actions besides commandment; further, that obedience and disobedience are more dependent on our interpretation of the intention of the one who commands than on our understanding of the law itself; and finally, that gospel as the declaration of divine action requires response no less than does commandment, though this response is not obedience but confidence and loyalty. On the other hand, the paradox of man-as-maker, dependent on the divine creator, is soluble, I think, when we reflect that all human making is also response to prior action and that the future-directed movement in human life is more eschatological than purely teleological. As eschatological it has a future in view that comes to us more than a future into which we go. On the whole, the difference between teleological and deontological practice and theory can be reduced—perhaps the two approaches may even be reconciled—if it is noted that both obedient man and man-the-maker are responders and that there are yet other ways of responding to action upon us besides these two. Nevertheless, my present intention is not to argue that the method of response-analysis is a more inclusive and fruitful approach to the Christian theory of human life than the standard approaches but rather to try to understand our existence in sin and salvation with its aid, putting aside the question of its greater applicability or the question whether it indeed offers opportunity for a more unified understanding of our ethos or only another, complementary way of dealing with ethical problems as Christians see them.

So regarded I see my human condition, my condition in selfhood rather, and that of my companions, as one of internal division and conflict because though I am one and though they are one in themselves, yet I and they are surrounded by many agencies, many systems of actions upon the self; these are diverse from each other, and to their actions the self makes unreconciled, ununified responses. In conventional religious language, in my sin I am a polytheist or polydemonist surrounded by, and reacting to, principalities and powers that rule in various domains. I am not subject indeed to attacks of multiple, atomic, disconnected actions beyond all possibility of interpretation. The actions are connected in systems, but the systems are not connected with each other. Some of the actions upon me I interpret as actions of nature, and I respond to them accordingly as a natural being, as man before nature; some I interpret as actions of my national society, and I respond to them as political being; some are the actions of biological drives or of the emotions connected with them, so that I respond as man before and in life. But the agencies that act upon me remain manifold and so am I manifold. I am I; I am one; yet I lack the actual integrity that is demanded by, or implicit in, my existence as a self.

> I have too many selves to know the one.
> In too complex a schooling was I bred,
> Child of too many cities who have gone
> Down all bright cross-roads of the world's desires,
> And at too many altars bowed my head
> To light too many fires.[2]

There is a law in me or in my mind, the law of my integrity; and there are many laws in my members, the laws of response to many systems of action about me. In my responsiveness and responsibility to the many I am irresponsible to One beyond the

[2] Eunice Tietjens, "A Plaint of Complexity," *Body and Raiment* (New York: Alfred A. Knopf, 1919), p. 13.

many; I am irresponsible as a self, however responsible the natural, the political, the domestic, the biological complexes in me may be in relation to the systems of nature, or to the closed societies of nation, church, family, or profession, or to the closed society of life itself.

I become more deeply involved in conflict within myself and in my world when I protest against this inner manifoldness by turning from the many systems of action upon me to myself. I undertake then to find myself within myself and to order myself and my surrounding world by beginning with my own actions, regarding all other actions as reactions only to my own primal deeds. Conflict with the others who surround me and who act similarly from themselves must now become the war of all against all. Conflict within myself ensues because I am a being of many interests, of many potential actions on my surrounding worlds of agents; I cannot identify myself with one of these sets of interests without calling forth the revolt of others. Manifoldness and conflict are not banished by this effort to flee from responsibility and responsiveness into a way of existence in which I act from myself only.

As it is with the self in itself so it is with the community of selves. The story of our communal life is the story of conflict and war and uneasy truces that hold off anarchy awhile. As flesh lusts against spirit and spirit against flesh within the self, so community lusts against community, nation against nation, church against state and state against church, religion against religion. Responsive and responsible to each other in our closed societies, we are irresponsible in the larger world that includes us all.

This state of sin, or of wretchedness and lostness, seems like the state to which the New Testament writers refer when they speak of man's subjection to principalities and powers and the rulers of the darkness of this world. Our mythology differs from theirs. We do not think of these systems as personal or anthropomorphic in character. Nevertheless they are systems, not human individuals nor atomic agencies. There is the system of nature, partly objective to us, partly historically subjective. It is the system of forces as known and interpreted by our society. It is powerful; it is heedless of our concerns; it is neither good nor evil. But we are in it and must adjust ourselves to it, be responsive to it. There are the systems of society, the customs and the mores, the large organizations of economic and cultural activities, all which are partly objective, partly subjective. We call them by such names as feudalism, industrialism, capitalism, communism, nationalism. There are vaguely defined ways of thinking, such as we sometimes call climates of opinion, or spirits of civilization. These also exercise dominion over us. Unquestioned, almost inaccessible assumptions in our common minds determine how we interpret and how we react. Or there are the complexes of emotions within us that largely determine how we accept and react to our fellow men, or, again, the manias that possess whole peoples for long periods—manias for possession or manias for poverty as in the early days of monasticism.

They are not all evil powers, not devils, with which we are concerned, though we may call some of them, with Walter Rauschenbusch, superpersonal forces of evil. But they are powers not identifiable with the willed influences of human groups or individuals. And they exercise dominion over us at least in this sense that we adjust our actions to them, do what fits into their action.

In this our personal and social manifoldness we have been left with a small seed of integrity, a haunting sense of unity and of universal responsibility. But there seems to be nothing in the world of forces acting upon us which makes that internal unity actual. There seems to be no One among all the many corresponding to that hidden self which is not free to act integrally amidst the many systems to which it responds.

From the point of view of reconciliation we say, however, that the One was and is always present to us even in our sin, but He or

"It" was and is present to us there as enemy. The natural mind is enmity to God; or to our natural mind the One intention in all intentions is animosity. In our wretchedness we see ourselves surrounded by animosity. We live and move and have our being in a realm that is not nothingness but that is ruled by destructive power, which brings us and all we love to nothing. The maker is the slayer; the affirmer is the denier; the creator is the destroyer; the life-giver is the death-dealer. There is indeed One intention in the light of which we interpret all the intentions of particular powers; there is One law of action that is present in all the specific laws of the systems that act upon us. We do respond to One action in all the many actions upon us, but that One in all the many is the *will* to destroy, or, if *will* be too anthromorphic a term, the *law* of our destruction. It is not the law of our physical dying only or primarily, but the law in things, the ontological law as it were, by which the self and its communities and all that it prizes, all its labors, worthy and unworthy, its good deeds and its evil ones, must be relativized, be restricted and finally come to nothing. In a thousand variations our religions, our poetry, our philosophies, our proverbial wisdom, bring home to us in this life from womb to grave, from war to war, the eschatological truth that "on us and all our race the slow, sure doom falls pitiless and dark"; that "all lovely things must have an ending, all lovely things must fade and die"; that "even this will pass away"; that "in the midst of life we are in death"; that those are happier who die young and those happiest who have never been born; that our physic "but prolongs . . . sickly days."

In the contradictoriness of our existence we do respond to One action present in all actions upon us. We do interpret all things that happen to us as occurring within One realm, as related to One intention so far as this life of selfhood and community is concerned. But the One beyond the many is the enemy, the creative source whence comes destruction. Hence the color of our lives is anxiety, and self-preservation is our first law. Hence we divide our world into the good and the evil, into friends who will assist us to maintain ourselves awhile and foes intent on our reduction to beings of no significance or to nothingness. Hence we develop all the religions that posit within the great animosity some kindly supernatural forces which will defend us, and we practice all sorts of rites of appeasement in order that the wrath may be turned away from us for awhile or that the mind of the One power may be changed so far as we or our communities are concerned, by exempting us from the universal rule of the law of coming to nothing.

When we confront an enemy we have three possible ways of reaction: ignoring, fighting, appeasing. In our lostness as selves before the One understood as enemy we may take these three attitudes in turn, or different members of the human community may represent the three attitudes. The courageous, aggressive attitude against such overwhelming power is rare among us, though those men are nearer to the knowledge of the One who defy him than are those who try to ignore him. Ignoring, forgetting, however, is the most usual attitude among us in our unreconciled existence. We turn to business as usual; we devote ourselves to the worship of all the little gods, to warfare with all the little destructive powers. We find meaning in dissociated systems of meaning. Pleasure for pleasure's sake; art for art's sake; truth for truth's sake. "The world is so full of a number of things, I'm sure we should all be happy as kings." We withdraw into the isolation of our little walled cities; we practice our special cults. Or thirdly we try appeasement. By the bringing of gifts, by special practices of discipline, by the offering of holocausts, by the cultivation of guilt-consciousness, by inflicting pain upon ourselves, we seek to turn away from ourselves the power of destruction aimed against us. The ways vary in religion and in our common life. But the interpretation we make of the One action that is present in all the many actions upon us and particularly present in the deed whereby we are, is always fundamentally the same one. The One power present in all powers is enemy. The maker is destroyer. In sin man lives before God—unknown as God, unknown as good, unrecognized as loveworthy and loving.

From the point of view of reconciliation we see that all our reactions to actions upon us have been and are qualified by this interpretation of the One realm in which all deeds occur, of the One limitation on all the time in which we act, and of the One agency present in all agencies. Defensiveness has entered into all our activity as makers; we have had to seek our own glory or that of our closed societies in all our construction, for otherwise no glory will be given. We have encountered every commandment with the suspicion that it was part of a code emanating in the last resort from inimical power jealous of our greatness, intent upon diminishing our human stature, desirous of keeping us unfree. Our pleasure-seeking and our self-seeking, our passionate devotion to limited causes that involved us in conflict with others equally passionate in their restricted loyalties—all these have roots in our understanding that there is an ultimate power with which we deal but that it is against us, desiring the death not only of the transgressor but also of the righteous, not only of the vicious but also of the virtuous. Hence all our righteousness in loyalty to finite societies or causes has been infected with anxiety, defensiveness, and hidden rebellion against the One.

This is the body of death, this network of interactions ruled by fear of God the enemy. This is the wretchedness of the human condition as we see it in the light of reconciliation. For salvation now appears to us as deliverance from that deep distrust of the One in all the many that causes us to interpret everything that happens to us as issuing ultimately from animosity or as happening in the realm of destruction. Redemption appears as the liberty to interpret in trust all that happens as contained within an intention and a total activity that includes death within the domain of life, that destroys only to re-establish and renew. Insofar as that interpretation prevails against its negative counterpart we begin to understand all that happens to us and to which we react as occurring in a final context of life-giving rather than death-dealing, as occurring in a universal teleology of resurrection rather than a universal teleology of entombment. Our response now is to commandments given with the promise of life rather than with the threat of death; it becomes response to action that holds before us the sure anticipation of glory—not our glory but the glory of all being. As all our actions of short-term or long-term purposiveness, of obedience or diso-bedience to the laws, were once shaped to fit into an interaction ending in destruction, they are now shaped—insofar as we are reconciled—into an interaction moving always toward universal, eternal life. The ethics of death is replaced by the ethics of life, of the open future, of the open society.

How this transition from God the enemy to God the friend is made in individual life and in the story of our human race is not the task of Christian ethics as ethics to set forth. For us who are Christians the possibility of making this new interpretation of the total action upon us by the One who embraces and is present in the many is inseparably connected with an action in our past that was the response of trust by a man who was sent into life and sent into death and to whom answer was made in his resurrection from the dead. Of that resurrection we may know no more than that he lives and is powerful over us and among us. We interpret the great sym-bolic, interpretative event in many ways with the aid of our various other symbols of purposiveness and of obedience. But however we fit it into the various schemes of rational understanding of this our life we must always say this about the event: "It reconciled and it reconciles us to God"; or otherwise, "In it God was reconciled." For after enemies are reconciled they no longer ask why it was that the animosity had developed in the past.

Through Jesus Christ, through his life, death, resurrection, and reign in power, we have been led and are being led to *metanoia*, to the reinterpretation of all our interpretations of life and death.

Death no less than life appears to us as act of mercy, not of mercy to *us* only, but in the great vicariousness of responsive and responsible existence, as mercy to those in whom, with whom, and for whom we live.

It is of course too much to say that the ethics of Christians is the ethics of the reconciled, or that their interpretations of life and death and neighbors have all passed through *metanoia*. For we who call ourselves by Christ's name recognize the presence in ourselves of the responses of distrust, of the ethics of death, as well as the movement toward life. In our biographies as in our human history the process of reconciliation has begun; at no point is it complete. Its completion is our hope and in this way our telos and our eschaton. That is one of the reasons why we do not know whether to call our self-interpretation Christian or simply human. Though we speak of our reconciliation to God, we share so much of the defensive, anxious, distrustful attitude toward being that we cannot put the common human ethics of unbelief in life on one side, as though it were something apart from us, as though its theory were unknown to us. And on the other hand we do not fail to note that among our companions who refuse to take the name of Christian responses to action are made that seem to be informed by the trust, the love of all being, the hope in the open future, that have become possible to us only in our life with Jesus Christ and in the presence of the One whom he encountered in all his encounters and to whom he gave fitting answer in all his answers to his companions. We believe that the reinterpretation of existence has come into the world and that it is not confined to those who say, "Lord, Lord," nor even necessarily best represented by them. But we have our responsible work to do in the church.

The responsible self we see in Christ and which we believe is being elicited in all our race is a universally and eternally responsive I, answering in universal society and in time without end, in all actions upon it, to the action of the One who heals all our diseases, forgives all our iniquities, saves our lives from destruction, and crowns us with everlasting mercy. The action we see in such life is obedient to law, but goes beyond all laws; it is form-giving but even more form-receiving; it is fitting action. It is action which is fitted into the context of universal, eternal, life-giving action by the One. It is infinitely responsible in an infinite universe to the hidden yet manifest principle of its being and its salvation.

APPENDIX

SELECTED PASSAGES
FROM THE
EARL LECTURES
ON
THE RESPONSIBLE SELF

AS THE PROLOGUE to the foregoing chapters makes clear, the approach that the author adopted for the Robertson Lectures could not, to his mind, be easily described as simply that of systematic theological ethics, for he sought to carry on his reflections not only in the milieu of Christian ethics as such but in the larger context of Western thought on moral man inclusive of both the classical philosophical and Christian traditions. The Earl Lectures, however, even though they treat of the same organizing images, exhibit the method and role of metaphor analysis more sharply and focus more directly on a Christian—though still universal—problematic. The explicit problem which the following selections from the Earl Lectures exemplify is the endeavor to bring the metaphor of responsibility into a more precisely articulated relation to the figure of Jesus Christ. The reader will find here, therefore, a series of paragraphs that at once presupposes and complements the train of thought laid down above and that suggests something more of the theological side of the program of H. R. Niebuhr's ethics, which would have received fuller elaboration in the book or books he had planned to write.

R. R. N.

A

METAPHORS AND MORALS

IN THE following [paragraphs] we shall attempt to interpret the
Christian life with the aid of the great modern symbol of responsibility. What is its form and character? How does it differ from other
styles of human existence and action? To what other styles is it
most closely related? How does the general Christian character and
form manifest itself in specific activities such as those in which
Christians, like all other people, engage when they marry and raise
children, eat and drink, obey civil laws and help enact them, when
they make material goods, buy and sell, participate in war and
peace-making; when they make all the countless daily evaluations,
decisions and choices that human beings must undertake in their
inescapable freedom? Our main attention, however, will not be
directed to such specific questions. We shall be concerned rather
with the style, or with the form, that comes to expression in specific
actions. We shall address ourselves to the question about our *being*

149

in the first place rather than about our *doing,* though it is certain
that in human existence being arises out of doing as well as that
doing manifests being.

Christian life is, at least, one of the distinctive ways of human
existence. Whether it is better or worse than other styles is a question neither Christians nor others are in a position to answer, since
men lack standards by which to judge their standards. At all events
the interpreter of the Christian life must resist the temptation to
substitute defense or evaluation for interpretation. As in all similar
situations defensiveness and self-justification tend to draw attention
away from the main task. They lead also to some misunderstanding
of the self, since when we are defensive we tend to magnify our
distinctiveness from others, and to undervalue our similarities and
agreements.

This has unfortunately been the case in Christianity when it interpreted itself of old in polemic or defensive confrontation with
Judaism or with the Greek philosophic life. It is our temptation
now when we tend to define ourselves vis-à-vis some styles of secu-
larist life, such as humanism. We cannot, to be sure, interpret without making distinctions and comparisons. But we can try to refrain
from the attempt to sit in judgment on our own cause, while we
seek to understand what we are and must try to be more fully.

A nondefensive effort at self-understanding may, moreover, have
the advantage of making our effort somewhat useful to fellow men
who do not count themselves Christians. To a very large extent, it
may be, Christianity represents a qualification of human practical
existence, or at least of Western moral life, rather than a new and
wholly different way of living; it may represent a species rather than
a genus of human moral existence. If that is true, as many before
us have believed, then the reflections of Christians on their life as
agents will to no small extent coincide with, or otherwise be similar
to, the reflections of some who are not Christians. The result may
be a kind of Christian philosophy of morals which will not only be

indebted to other philosophies but, hopefully, may make some contributions to them.

ON SYMBOLIC FORMS AS A KEY TO MORAL UNDERSTANDING

I propose that we undertake to reflect on our life as moral selves in general, as Christians in particular, with the aid of contemporary ideas about the nature and the role of symbolic forms. These ideas have been made familiar to us by many students of human life and action but have not yet been widely used in those inquiries we generally designate by the name of ethics.

The idea of symbolic forms has been in part suggested by the work of psychologists who have called attention to the manner in which both in dreams and in other more or less unconscious production we express deep-rooted desires, fears, and conflicts in pictures and dramas that disguise as well as reveal the sources of their inspiration. In this case we are dealing with images and stories that need to be interpreted.

But there is another line of investigation into symbols which is more significant for the moralist. This is the line of thought persuasively presented and amply illustrated by that philosophy of symbolic forms which Ernst Cassirer developed. He was preceded in this effort by many students of special provinces, such as those of language and of art. He has been followed by many inquirers in these and other fields of human experience and expression. Gestalt-psychology and the psychology of perception in general have made their own parallel or dependent contributions to this way of man's self-understanding.

What is the general idea in such interpretation of ourselves as *symbolic* more than as *rational·* animals? It is, I believe, this: that we are far more image-making and image-using creatures than we usually think ourselves to be and, further, that our processes of perception and conception, of organizing and understanding the signs that come to us in our dialogue with the circumambient world, are guided and formed by images in our minds. Our languages, we are reminded, are symbolic systems. Their very structures, their allocation of names to parts of our experience, their verbs, their tenses, their cases, their grammar and syntax, contain systems of forms with which we come to the multiplicity or chaos of our encounter with things. With the aid of these symbolic systems we distinguish and relate our pasts, presents, and futures; we divide up the world of nature into apprehendable, graspable entities; we relate these to each other in patterns that are intelligible and somehow manageable. The words we use in any language, moreover, are so richly metaphorical that we cannot even speak about metaphors or try to limit their use without employing metaphors. Even when we speak about *literal* meanings we use a metaphor. Consider John Locke's sober statement about figurative speeches and allusions, allowable in his view only when we seek pleasure or delight but not information: ". . . all the *artificial* and *figurative applications* of words eloquence hath *invented,* are for nothing else but to *insinuate* wrong ideas, *move* the *passions,* and thereby *mislead* the judgment; and so indeed are *perfect cheats.*"[1] He was unable to convey this information about figures of speech without making use of nine or ten figures of speech or metaphorical words.

The study of language as a symbolic system, whether in its highly specialized forms of scientific and poetic languages, or in its "common sense" forms, is probably the primary source of our undrestanding of man as symbolic animal, but it is not the only one.

The evidence of the historians of art is also impressive. They call attention to the way in which pictorial representation in various periods not only mirrors but guides men's changing apprehensions of actuality. How differently the Egyptian saw the human face and the varieties of human classes from the way the Greek saw them is indicated by their pictorial art, but it is probable that art also guided

[1] *An Essay Concerning Human Understanding,* ed. A. C. Fraser (Oxford: Clarendon Press, 1894), Bk. III, Chap. X, § 34. (Italics are H.R.N.'s.—Ed.)

the seeing.[2] What is true of painting and sculpture may be even truer of poetry, drama, and novel. The representation of human life in the Homeric epic on the one hand and in the Hebrew sacred story on the other tell us not only that the symbolic forms of expression of different peoples were different but that their apprehensions of nature and of human life were different and that these apprehensions were guided by the simple or complex images with which they came to nature and to fellow men.[3] The history of religions, again, brings into view the manifoldness and diversity, but also the indispensability of symbolism in all man's experience, apprehension, and interpretation of the holy or the supernatural, or of the final circumambiency in which he lives and moves and has his being. That religion and art are highly symbolic we have long known, but the symbolic character of science and philosophy has only recently been called to our attention. Now we understand, for instance, what a mighty though often unacknowledged role in guiding scientific experiment and theory during the last three hundred years the image of the machine has played and how the symbol of the mathematical system has impressed itself on the scientific mind and been impressed by it on the phenomena it undertakes to isolate, study, and interpret. And so with metaphysics the root-metaphors of generating substance, of the republic, of the organism, of the machine, of the event, and of the mathematical system have exercised a deep-going influence on the construction of the great systems which those great artists, the metaphysical philosophers, have set before us as images of being itself.[4]

Man as language-user, man as thinker, man as interpreter of nature, man as artist, man as worshiper, seems to be always sym-

[2] Cf. E. H. J. Gombrich, *Art and Illusion* (New York: Pantheon Books, 1961).

[3] Erich Auerbach, *Mimesis,* trans. W. R. Trask (New York: Oxford University Press, 1953), Chap. I.

[4] Cf. Stephen Pepper, *World Hypotheses* (Berkeley: University of California Press, 1961).

bolic man, metaphor-using, image-making, and image-using man. What then about man as moral, man as deciding between goods, as evaluating man, as self-defining, self-creating man, as the judge of conduct in its rightness and wrongness? Is man in this activity also the symbolic animal? Since man as moral agent is present in all his activities it would seem likely that in his total decision-making and the administration of all his affairs he would be no less symbolic than he is in any one of them.

THE SYMBOLIC FORM OF JESUS CHRIST

At all events when we reflect on our existence as Christians with this hypothesis in mind we become aware that in Christian life Jesus Christ is a symbolic form with the aid of which men tell each other what life and death, God and man, are *like;* but even more he is a form which they employ as an a priori, an image, a scheme or pattern in the mind which gives form and meaning to their experience. This is not to say that the symbolic form is projected, as though there were no reality except that which is in the mind. It is to say that in the dialogue of the self and other, of subject and object, the questions put by the subject in part determine the answer, though the question has arisen out of previous dialogue and the answer affects the next question.

How Jesus Christ, his *Gestalt,* his drama, function as symbolic forms in Christian thinking about God, the long history of theology no less than the immediate religious language of the New Testament brings to our attention. But we are now concerned with the role of this symbol in the life of agents, who value and disvalue, who judge and respond to judgment, who decide, and react to decisions made about them. And there we note first of all how much there has entered into the moral language of Christians the figure of Jesus Christ. They know themselves to be Christians when they see their companions in need in the form of Christ; there echoes in their memories in such moments the story Christ told which ended in the well-known statement, "Inasmuch as you have done it to one of the least of these my brethren you have done it unto me." The symbol is not a mere figure of speech. Symbol and reality participate in each other. The needy companion is not wholly other than Christ, though he is not Christ himself. He is a Christo-morphic being, apprehended as in the form of Christ, something like Christ, though another.

Because Jesus Christ is symbolic form, Christians can say with Studdert-Kennedy, "All through life I see a cross, where sons of men give up their breath. There is no gain except by loss; there is no life except by death." With the use of the symbolic form of Jesus Christ, the Christian—consciously or unconsciously—apprehends, interprets, and evaluates his fellow man. The identification may be more or less complete, more or less conscious. When it is least conscious it may, indeed, be most effective. It seems even true that the symbol is highly effective among many men who are not consciously Christian at all.

As with the apprehension, understanding, and evaluation of the fellow man so it is with the apprehension or the understanding of God, or of the last giver of commandments to life, or of the final goal of the human quest after the vision of glory, or of the last activity to which the self responds. Jesus Christ is the symbolic figure without which the Christian can no longer imagine, or know, or believe in the Determiner of Destiny, or the final end, or the ultimate source, or the last environment to which he is related in all his relations, though he stops short of identifying symbol and actuality. Jesus Christ, too, is the symbolic figure with which he understands or apprehends the ultimate spirit that moves in the depths of his life and of all creation. He tests the spirits to see if among all the forces that move within him, his societies, the human mind itself, there be a uniting, a healing, a knowing, a whole-making spirit, a Holy Spirit. And he can do so only with the aid of the image, the symbol of Christ. "Is there a Christ-like spirit there?"

Again Jesus Christ is the symbolic form with which the self understands itself, with the aid of which it guides and forms itself in its actions and its sufferings. Paul's statement, "It is no longer I that live but Christ who lives within me," runs almost to the extreme of identification. Less extreme are all the symbolic statements of those Christians who think of and, in part, conduct their lives as imitations of Christ, as conformities to his mind; who follow him, are his disciples, live, suffer, and die with him.

It is impossible to describe with any adequacy the variety and richness of the imagery derived by Christians from the story of Jesus and employed by them not only in their descriptive language but in their apprehensions, evaluations, and decisions. From the recognition of an infant's value and destiny with the aid of images of manger and cross of Christ, to the acceptance of death as a dying with Christ, to the discovery of a quality of existence that like Christ's cannot be conquered by death, to the understanding of man's place and responsibility in the cosmos as a son of God, the symbolism of the gospel story pervades the Christian consciousness in all evaluation, action, and suffering.

To insist in this fashion on the symbolic function of the Christ-figure and the Christ-story does not beg the question of the historical actuality of that figure and story. For history may function as myth or as symbol when men use it (or are forced by processes in their history itself to employ it) for understanding their present and their future. When we grasp our present, not so much as a product of our past, but more as essentially revealed in that past, then the historical account is necessarily symbolic; it is not merely descriptive of what was once the case. Thus, we observe today how in America the story of the Civil War functions among us symbolically without ceasing to be historic; with its aid we apprehend the structures of our national, historical existence, as North and South, as black and white, as agrarian and industrial; we also discern the tragedy of the judgment that lies on us in past and present and the grandeur of

sacrifice and courage that appears in the midst of this guilty existence. But this is not the place to explore the relations of history and
myth, or of actuality and symbol. It must suffice us to note that for
Christians it is at least as important to reject the thought that Jesus
Christ is only an historical figure as it is to deny that he is only a
symbol. (The phrase "only a symbol" usually betrays lack of
understanding of the power and importance of symbolic forms in
our lives, since symbols are essential ingredients of the world in
which we live. Without symbols nothing has intelligibility and form
for us. Without them we grope in darkness.)

More important in this context than the question about the relation of history and symbol is the question about the relations of the
Christ-symbol to other symbolic forms which we bring to the understanding and the shaping of our existence as agents. Is the Christ
symbol the only or the wholly dominant and completely adequate
form for Christians, or is it always associated with other symbols
so that it is impossible for Christians to define themselves simply
as Christians? Similar questions have been raised in the past in
other ways as when it was asked whether Christian morality presupposed a common human morality, or whether Christian law
presupposed natural law, or whether gospel presupposed law. Practically, the problem often presents itself as one about the Christian's
concern with a social morality that is not pervaded by the Christ-
symbol. But we must attempt to get at this set of problems with the
aid of our heuristic device—the philosophy of symbolic forms.

Now it is doubtless true that we cannot interpret the Christian
life without reference to the Christ-symbol. There would be no
meaning in calling it Christian life or in distinguishing it from Jewish or Roman or democratic or some other form, if we did not attend to the significance in it of Jesus Christ as a fundamental, indispensable metaphor. But the question is whether we can understand
ourselves and our companions in Christianity or in Christendom,
whether we can and do give form to our active existence, with this

as our only symbol? In most periods of history there have been Christians who have made the attempt to make Jesus Christ not only the exclusive principle of their understanding but also of their action. But they have never succeeded in doing so, for they have always actually employed other symbolic forms besides. Sometimes they derived these from a Scripture that contains many other words and conveys many other symbolic forms besides this one. Otherwise they derived them from the culture they shared with non-Christians. In our time the effort to achieve a completely Christocentric and solely Christo-morphic form of thinking and acting has been confined to theology, most notably to Karl Barth's theology. But actually in such theology, as in the case of the exclusive Christian communities of the past, other symbols have had to be employed if the symbol of Christ was to be used. Barth, to take this representative of the most consistent Christian symbolism as our example, attempts to dismiss all analogies, all metaphors, all symbols from Christian speech and conduct except Jesus Christ. But, of course, he cannot interpret the meaning of Jesus Christ without the aid of other metaphors and symbols such as Word of God, Son of God, Servant, Lord, covenant, humiliation, exaltation, reconciliation, salvation. Particularly in speech about Christian ethics he must employ non-Christian though not non-Biblical symbols, such as commandment, law, obedience, and permission.

The situation of Christians then seems to be this: they cannot understand themselves or direct their actions or give form to their conduct without the use of the symbol Jesus Christ, but with the aid of that symbol only they never succeed in understanding themselves and their values or in giving shape to their conduct. And, furthermore, the problem of the adequacy, the revelatory value, of the symbols they associate with Jesus Christ is often as great as the problem of the revelatory value of the Christ symbol itself. In our time the question of the general symbols we must employ for the understanding of our existence as agents seems as acute as the question about the Christian symbol itself. Man's moral self-understanding is full of problems. Hence when we ask whether a new general symbolic form is arising in our culture, namely the root-metaphor of responsibility, we are asking a double question. Are we finding a new symbolic form through which to understand Jesus Christ as well as a new form through which to understand ourselves, and so a new form in which to understand ourselves in our relation to Christ?

THE ROOT-METAPHORS OF HISTORIC CHRISTIAN ETHICS

Before we raise the question about responsibility, however, we shall need to call to mind the main types of general moral symbolism we have used in the past, and still largely use today. This is a symbolism Christians have shared with the societies in and with which they have lived. In those societies men in isolating, defining, understanding, directing, explaining their life as agents, their moral existence, have made a manifold use of simile, metaphor, and symbol. They have, in general, used synecdoche, that is, they have apprehended their total activity and their total existence as agents with the aid of some one of their many activities as representative of all. They have said the whole is like one of its parts; they have then analyzed the part and have interpreted the whole in the light of that analysis.

Many partial activities have been used to interpret the whole. The active life of man has been understood as being *like* warfare, and then indeed been *symbolized* by, and even *identified* with, a warfare in which the enemies are not physical. In Zoroastrian ethics, it seems likely, the image of war has become much more than a simile; it seems to function there as symbolic form. In our West it is not a dominant symbolic form, but the image does function symbolically, as when we experience internal conflicts or racial antagonisms, or fight against temptation. We use the image of our journeyings toward destinations as pictures of what we are and what we are doing in all action. And these similes can also become symbols when our lives become pilgrimages, move toward personal, national, or human goals, or when we designate our ethos as the American, or the Western, or the Christian, or even the Presbyterian or Methodist *way* of life. From commerce we derive first similes, then symbols, of indebtedness to one another, of punishment as a payment of debt to society, of contract, of giving every man his due, and perhaps even of all moral existence as an affair of duties.

Two great synecdoches, however, have established themselves in our Western world, as symbolic forms with the aid of which we not only interpret a given actuality but define its limits and apprehend its structure. What are we attending to when we attend to the moral life, or to the life of selves as agents? What are we talking about when we converse with one another on the subject? What is it that we are attempting to deal with practically in ourselves and in others? We are attending, according to the one great symbol, to all that life and action of ours which is like our craftsmanship, which is indeed and yet not quite a craftsmanship. We are attending, according to the other great symbol, to all that activity of ours which is like our political action of obeying and giving laws. For the sake of brevity, we shall call the first symbol that of *homo faber,* the second that of *homo politicus.* To these two great dominant symbols a third is being gradually added in our modern world, the symbol of responsibility—or to give it a Latin name, the symbol of *homo dialogicus*—but that is a story we shall reserve for [another] lecture.

B

Responsibility and Christ

OUR EFFORT in these lectures is directed toward understanding the Christian manner or way or style of life. We are not trying to defend or to recommend but only to understand it as best we can. Our method has been derived largely from the philosophy of symbolic forms which sees man as symbolic animal. He is a being who grasps and shapes reality, including the actuality of his own existence, with the aid of great images, metaphors, and analogies. These are partly in his conscious mind but so largely in his unconscious mind and in the social language that he tends to take them for granted as forms of pure reason. They are, indeed, forms of reason, but of historic reason. Thus man thinks of things anthropomorphically, or mechanomorphically, or mathematico-morphically, without always being aware that his patterns are not copies of the reality to which he reacts but products of an art of knowing in which subject and object interact. His conceptual systems, accordingly, are largely abstractions from his symbolic forms.

Our first argument was that Christians in their interpretations of human life and in the administration of their own existences always employ the symbolic form of Jesus Christ—that is what makes them Christians. But with this symbol they usually associate not only many minor symbols such as those of pilgrimage, healing, warfare, etc. but also as a rule some other grand image of the world and of human life. So we argued that Western Christians have employed two great metaphors of the moral life in conjunction with the Christ-symbol: those of man-the-maker, or realizer of ideals, and of man-the-citizen, the obeyer and enacter of laws. The argument above was that a third great symbolic form is becoming available for self-interpretation; that this form, as the history of moral language and of our nonmoral inquiries indicate, is perhaps becoming dominant over the older forms; that, at least, it is supplying us with an additional perspective. And so we undertook to conceptualize or to analyze the elements implicit in the symbol of *responsibility*.[1]

Now a third task is before us. With the aid of this clarified picture of ourselves as responsible beings, we must try to understand Christians as selves who in all their actions answer to alterations on the basis of their interpretations of such alterations, whose responses are meant to fit into the whole relevant pattern of alteraction and interaction, who make their responses also in accountability, that is in anticipation of answers to their answers. How can Christians relate the form of Christ to the form of responsibility? Or how do we understand ourselves as both responsible in our Christianity and Christian in our responsibility?

CHRIST AS PARADIGM OF RESPONSIBILITY[2]

There are doubtless as many ways of associating Jesus Christ with the responsible life as there have been ways of associating him with the ideal life or the obedient or dutiful one. And it is only an

[1] Cf. Chap. I, above.
[2] Section heading supplied by editor.

old, though deeply established, prejudice which will lead us to believe that there is only one fitting answer to the question, one ideal solution of the problem, one right relationship. "God fulfills himself in many ways lest one good custom should corrupt the earth." A theory of ethics must not be confused with a life decision or with an absolute imperative. Decisions have a kind of exclusive validity; once we have decided that a certain act is right or good or fitting we must proceed and accept the consequences for ourselves. A theory, however, is not such a personal decision. We commit ourselves to a theory only tentatively. The imperative in it is only hypothetical. With this warning to ourselves not to take ourselves too seriously we can decide to proceed nevertheless and make a resolute effort to understand Christian life in terms of responsibility.

In the older theories of Christian idealism and of Christian obedience Jesus Christ usually functions in a double way, as prophet and as priest, or as king and as priest. On the one hand he appears as the perfect illustration or the incarnate pattern, as the first and only Christian. On the other hand his personal, historical action is understood as God's way of making what is impossible for men possible. Christ makes it possible for men to participate in his kind of life, to become somewhat like Christ despite the vast disparity between a unique son of God and all the prodigal children of the Almighty. Thus he is understood as man, perfectly directed toward God as his end, or perfectly obedient to the Father; and he is acknowledged as divine, as the power of God or as act or Word of God that redirects men who had lost their relation to their end, become enslaved to false goals or had fallen into disobedience. In whatever form we interpret Christian ethics, in it Christ always has something of this double character. In him man is directed toward God; in him also God is directed toward men. Hence the Christian ethos is that of a community which knows through reason and through Jesus Christ what it and man in general should make out of life, or what law ought to be obeyed, and how; or what goal chosen; it also knows man's lack of power to undertake such a construction, pursue such a pilgrimage, or be obedient to such a will and law; finally, it is a community that finds itself driven to attempt what lies beyond man's strength and to persist hopefully in a hopeless journey toward the unattainable goal that Christ attained, to attempt an obedience that is ever in need of forgiveness; yet forgiven it attempts again to obey. That is the empowerment it receives from Christ.

(This duality of the function of Christ in the Christian life seems largely responsible for the difficulties Christians encounter in relating their ethics to the ethics of the philosophers—a problem which we cannot pursue at this time.)

When we look at the Jesus Christ of the New Testament story and as he exists symbolically in the Christian consciousness, from the point of view of responsibility, we note a similar duality of function. First of all, he is the responsible man who in all his responses to alterations did what fitted into the divine action. He interpreted every alteration that he encountered as a sign of the action of God, of the universal, omnificent One, whom he called Father. He responded to all action upon him as one who anticipated the divine answer to his answers. Will of God meant for him not only or primarily divine imperative but the divine action, carried out through many agencies besides those of men obedient to commandment. To pray, "Thy will be done in earth as it is in heaven," did not evidently mean "Make us obedient," though that petition may be implied. The Gethsemane prayer, "Not my will but thine be done," did not refer to commandments but to acts of God that were to be carried out by men who did not inquire about the will of God. The statement, "It is not the will of the Father that one of these little ones should perish," seems to refer to what God does as much as to what he requires human agents to do. The will of God is what God does in all that nature and men do. It is the universal that contains and transforms, includes and fashions, every particular. Will of God is present for Jesus in every event from the death of sparrows, the shining of sun and descent of rain, through the exercise of authority by ecclesiastical and political powers that abuse their authority, through treachery and desertion by disciples, to the impending beleaguerment of Jerusalem and the end of the aeon. All this interpretation of every alteraction as included in, or as taken up by, the action of God was neither fatalistic nor mechanical. The idea that all acts of finite agents had been predesigned, as though God were the author of a play in which each actor played a predestined role, is remote from Jesus' way of thinking. The Universal One whom he calls Father is Lord of heaven and earth. His action is more like that of the great wise leader who uses even the meannesses of his subjects to promote the public welfare.

Let us take a few examples of Jesus' interpretation of alteraction, that is to say, of the kinds of finite events to which all men respond in one way or another in accordance with their interpretations of what these events mean. Consider how he interprets natural happenings, those acts occurring in the natural environment which are important elements in every human ethos, since we are always reacting to them in accordance with our interpretations. We see them as parts of a large pattern; we read them as words in a sentence which get their meaning from the whole sentence. What is the large pattern, what the inclusive action to which Jesus responds with his evaluations and other actions, when he encounters a natural event? He sees as others do that the sun shines on criminals, delinquents, hypocrites, honest men, good Samaritans, and VIP's without discrimination, that rains come down in equal proportions on the fields of the diligent and of the lazy. These phenomena have been for unbelief, from the beginning of time, signs of the operation of a universal order that is without justice, unconcerned with right and wrong conduct among men. But Jesus interprets the common phenomena in another way: here are the signs of cosmic generosity. The response to the weather so interpreted leads then also to a response to criminals and outcasts, who have not been cast out by the infinite

Lord. So it is also with carefree birds who deserve no pay for useful work, and with flowers that have done no heroic deeds to merit their colorful ribbons and brilliant medals. Are these appearances to be interpreted as signs that the power of life expressed in natural things is unconcerned with the quality of what issues from it? Or are they to be understood as signs of the presence of an overflowing creativity, of an infinite artistry, that rejoices in its creations, that rejects, because it is all grace, the censorships of human laws, not because it falls below the common human standard, but rises far above it? There is a righteousness of God for Jesus; there is a universal ordering for good; but it is different in all its working from the provincial, even planetary righteousness that men have discovered or devised. Thus he understands and reacts to natural events as expressive of an omnificent intention that is wholly affirmative of what it brings into being.

What is true of the extrahuman, natural world is true of the human. To children, whose angels behold the face of the Father who is in heaven, to sinners who are also the children of Abraham, to the sick and lost whose salvation is to be to the glory of God— to all these he responds as having a meaning derived from their place in that divine action, which hates nothing that it has made but wills it to be and to be whole.

In his responses also to the limiting and destructive actions to which he is subject, Jesus acts as one who interprets them in the context of divine, of universal, action. He reads these signs also as words in a divine sentence. He responds to the infinite intention, behind or inclusive of all the finite intentions. He understands that Pilate would have no power over him had it not been granted to the procurator from above. He pronounces woes on his betrayer, yet the son of man goes as it has been determined, not by betrayer but by the will beyond all finite wills. So it is also with those words and actions of Jesus that relate to the coming end of his time or of the aeon, which occasion much difficulty to those interpreters of his ethical sayings who use idealistic or legal patterns of interpretation. The significance of eschatology in the gospels lies for them in the fact that the time is short before the consummation of all things. Hence the telos is confused by an eschaton, the normal law by a law for the interim. But the evident weight in these sayings about the future does not lie on the time-factor so much as on the God-factor. The divine rule, the divine action in all things, which now men only dimly perceive and understand in their encounter with creative and destructive events, will be clearly revealed at last, in the end. What is to become clear in the end, however, is not something new. It is now an emergency that is coming. The actuality of the present is to become emergent. God whose rule is hidden and whose rule will become manifest is ruling now, despite all hiddenness. Realized eschatology is realized theology.

If then we try to summarize the ethos of Jesus in a formula we may do so by saying that he interprets all actions upon him as signs of the divine action of creation, government, and salvation and so responds to them as to respond to divine action. He does that act which fits into the divine action and looks forward to the infinite response to his response.

The Christian ethos so uniquely exemplified in Christ himself is an ethics of universal responsibility. It interprets every particular event as included in universal action. It is the ethos of citizenship in a universal society, in which no being that exists and no action that takes place is interpretable outside the universal context. It is also the ethos of eternal life, in the sense that no act of man in response to action upon him does not involve repercussions, reactions, extending onward toward infinity in time as well as in social space.

As ethos of universal responsibility the ethos exemplified in Jesus Christ is not unique. It has affinities to other forms of universal ethics. Insistence on the absolute uniqueness of the Christian ethos has never been able to meet either the theoretical or the practical test. In practice, Christians undertaking to act in some fashion in conformity with Christ find themselves doing something like what some others, conforming to other images, are doing. Identity of action there has not been; likeness, however, has often been present. (Christians have had no monopoly on humanitarianism or concern for those suffering deprivation; in reverence for life they have often been excelled by others.) On the theoretic side, when Christians have undertaken to set forth the pattern present in the action of Christ they have found kinship between it and certain patterns of moral conduct set forth by universalist philosophers, that is, by thinkers who saw man first of all as a citizen of the universe, as endowed with a reason that seeks universal truth, as subject to laws that are unversal. For the most part these affinities of the Christian ethos with other types of universal ethics have been stated in terms of idealism or of legalism, as when Platonic or Aristotelian ethics on the one hand, Kantian thought or universal utilitarianism on the other, have been associated with Christian ethics.

If we try to state such affinities in terms of responsibility ethics our attention is directed toward the kinship of Christian with Jewish ethics on the one hand, with Stoicism on the other. There may be some sense but there is also evidently much nonsense in what many Christians have said about the legalistic character of Hebrew and Jewish ethics. It is significant that they themselves when they use the Scriptures as a sourcebook of ethics, a guide to conduct, turn to the Hebrew Scriptures, especially to the prophets and the Psalms, not only as writings which point beyond themselves to Christ but as books that give concreteness and filling to the ethos exemplified in Jesus. One may even say that the Old Testament fulfills the New for them in practice, and not only the New the Old. In the prophetic writings particularly they find an ethos of universal responsibility expressed and enacted; but it is present elsewhere too. One may take as an example of responsibility to the one and universal God the kind of thinking presented in the Joseph story and summarized in Joseph's statement to his brothers: "You thought to do evil but God thought to do good, to bring it about that many people should be kept alive." Here the clear distinction is made between the particular intentions that guide a finite action and the divine intention that uses or lies behind such actions. So Joseph can and does forgive, responding to the infinite in his reaction to the finite. There is no legalism in that sort of thinking. It seems to be a case of interpretation and response more than of obedience to a law or of goal-seeking. Another clear paradigm of the ethics of response to divine action behind, in, and through all finite activity is found in the tenth chapter of Isaiah. The problem presented for human decision in this chapter has something, but not too much, to do with obedience to the law. It is the problem of how to meet an emergency—in this case an Assyrian invasion. How is this alteration to be met? What is the fitting response to this emergency? What the prophet offers is first of all an interpretation of what is going on. The invasion is to be understood, as he makes quite clear, as act of God. Israel is to ask, What is *God* doing? The divine intention Isaiah points out is directed toward the purgation or the chastisement of Israel. Israel is therefore to forget all its stereotyped interpretations of such encounters as attacks of the ungodly on the godly. It is itself the godless people that must be reformed, called back to its covenants, to its own laws and ways of justice. But this divine intention, says the prophet, is to be radically distinguished from the intentions of Assyria and its leaders, who are godless, too, though in another way. The destructive intentions of Assyria are one thing; the holy, saving intentions of God are another. The meet, the fitting response of Israel, must be to the infinite intention in the first place, to the finite intention only secondarily. That means that the first response, the fitting action in the critical hour, is to be internal reformation; defense against Assyria is the secondary thing.

The chapter represents, it seems to me, the logic of Hebrew

ethics as that ethics runs through all the pages of Hebrew Scriptures and through the tragic, yet wonderful story of this people of God. It is an ethos of laws, to be sure, but an ethos which centers even more in responsiveness to omnificence, to the all-doer. There is no evil in the city but the Lord has done it. No nation exists that he has not called into being. It is he that besets man behind and before and lays his hand upon him; from him no flight is possible though one makes one's home in Sheol. To discern the ways of God not in supernatural but in all natural and historic events, to respond to his intention present in and beyond and through all finite intentions, that is the way of responsibility to God. It is a way of universal responsibility because there is no action in the whole extent of actuality in which the universal intention, the meaning of the One beyond the many, is not present.

Of course this is a Christian's interpretation of Israelite ethos. But it is that of a Christian who is indebted to the Jew, because his Christ was a Jew; who must understand his Christ with the aid of the Hebrew Scriptures; and who, when he asks what God is intending now in preserving this people against Christian and pseudo-Christian and pagan attacks, must answer: They are given to us for a sign; they point us to universal responsibility. They are, whatever their own intentions may be, our saviors from a polytheism into which we Gentile nations are forever tempted to fall.

A second type of ethos with which the Christian has historical and theoretically describable affinities is that of Stoicism. Stoic ethics, though variously described, seems most intelligible when regarded as an ethics of response. The Stoics are concerned with *nomos* and with the ideal life of apathy, or serenity. But primarily they deal with the ways men react, wisely or foolishly, to the things that befall them, to the things that are not in their power, to pain and pleasure, good and evil fortune. To respond to these things with passion is to react without understanding, without wisdom, without humanity. The secret of the wise life is its recognition of the presence in all events of universal Nature, of "creative, cosmic power, the world-thought," the world-reason. When birth and death and the things that happen to life between these terminal points are understood as outworkings of the world-reason, or of God, as the later Stoics said, then the wise man will do the fitting thing, the act that is in accord with the working of the universal reason. Stoic action is action in the universe; it is not dominated by the concerns of a single, individual life, nor yet by those of some special group. The Stoic is a citizen of the cosmos to whom nothing is foreign that is not foreign to the central, all-pervading power; he looks to every event as expressive in some fashion of universal plan and pattern; he interprets it in that way and so tries to respond fittingly. When early Christians, seeking to develop a social ethics in the Roman world, adopted much Stoic thought, and even classified Seneca with the fathers as St. Seneca, they showed a sound instinct for the affinity of one universal ethos with another.

In Spinoza a special form of such Stoic universal ethics is developed. He sees the human problem as one of enslavement by those fuzzy, inadequate, and self-centered ideas which lead man to interpret whatever happens to him in terms of its apparent beneficence or maleficence toward his personal private self and so to react with emotion. Deliverance comes through a universalized interpretation of what is happening.

To many a Christian it is a far cry from Epictetus and Spinoza to the gospels and epistles of the New Testament. But let them remember how much greater is the distance to the latter from all those styles of life that are developed by men who live in a world in which all events outside the limited sphere of man's domain are the results of the collisions of blindly running atoms, or of the acts of little gods that rule in partiality over small areas. Instead of distinguishing between styles of life by contrasting the search for happiness with the search for virtue, or by contrasting obedience to natural, rational law with obedience to revealed law, we shall do

well, I think, to mark the lines of division that run between egoisms of every kind, social, closed-society ethics of every sort, and
the universalisms, whether these be presented to us as ethics of
aspiration after universal good, or of obedience to universal law,
or of responsibility in universal society, to universal power.

There is an egoistic style of life, even one which calls itself
Christian, but has nothing in common with what we see in Jesus
Christ, since it seeks only its own happiness and interprets whatever happens to it as action of a God whose only concern is just
with this lonely self, a God who is the counterpart of individuality, not the Lord of being. There is also a social style which lives
in an enclave in the universe; when this appears in Christian form
the enclave is a Christian church, which participates in a special
history—and which finds divine action really only in the creation,
government, and salvation of that special society of the elect. Such
ethics indeed has little in common with Stoic or Spinozistic uni-
versalism. It has much in common with every kind of closed-society
ethics. But the ethics of Jesus Christ, as the way of life of one who
responds to the action of the universal God in all action, in whatever happens, is an ethics of universal responsibility and not wholly
alien to all those styles of life that men have developed when they
lifted up their eyes beyond the particularities of their situation and
looked for the universal good beyond all special goods, the universal law beyond all local law, the universal action beyond all
particular action.

Before we now proceed to ask how Jesus Christ works in the
Christian consciousness in a second way, we need to answer one
evident objection to the foregoing sketch of his ethics. Does not
this way of understanding him, and so of understanding the model
Christian life, make of this life an affair of pure resignation to the
will of God? Is not this interpretation one of fatalism? One answer
to this objection is that submission to determination in the form

in which it is represented, for instance, by Islam, may be less foreign to the Christianity of Jesus Christ than is all the ethics of absolute human freedom, the ethics of man the conqueror of the conditions in which he lives, the ethics of human mastery. More important, however, is the question how the determining power, the One who acts in all the many, is understood. When this One is understood, with the use of the symbols of making and of design, as the predesigner, the foreordainer of all that happens, then indeed nothing but fatalism could result from an ethics of response to God. Then Judas' treachery is predesigned, and then Russia's attack on the West is foreordained, and you and I play out the roles which have been written down for us in the script. But such a Determiner of Destiny is not the One to whom Jesus Christ made his responses; nor is he the God of Isaiah; nor would he be One to whom we have access. The God and Father of our Lord Jesus Christ is the loving dynamic One, who does new things, whose relation to his world is more like that of father to his children than like that of the maker to his manufactures; it is more like that of the ruler to his realm than like that of the designer to his machines. The symbols fatalism uses to interpret what is happening do not fit the situation. The [images] of the kingdom and of the family are, to be sure, symbols also, but they do greater justice to our actual experience of life. They fit this dialogue in which our free acts take place in response to actions over which we have no power, in which our free acts are not truly *ours,* and free, unless they are the consequences of interpretation. They fit the dialogue also in which our free actions can never be freed from the responses that will be made to them. Our freedom presupposes and anticipates action not subject to our control. To think of the determination to which we are so subject as in itself invariant after the manner of a machine is to become enslaved by an erroneous myth. Since we shall in any case use myths, let us use our myths critically and with discrimination.

CHRIST AS REDEEMER TO RESPONSIBLE BEING[3]

We have noted that the meaning of Jesus Christ for the Christian life, no matter what interpretative aid is brought to him, is almost always a double one. In the much criticized Ritschlian theology and ethics of the nineteenth century this dual role was most evident. Christ was the perfect man, the moral emergent, the revealer in word and conduct of the ideal, the proclaimer and realizer of the Kingdom of God or of the realm of ends. He belonged in the history of evolutionary morals at the apex. He was also the savior who set faltering, stumbling, guilty men, forever transgressing their own moral law, back on their feet; who gave the hope of victory to those who despaired because of their many defeats. He not only gave an example to the life of the human spirit; he not only realized in himself the potentiality, slowly actualized before him, of personal existence. He also rescued that spirit from death; he resurrected it, healed it, and continued by his priestly work to do so.

The duality so expressed in Ritschlian formulation has been expressed in other ways in other theories and conceptions of the Christian life, as we have previously noted. Christ is the man in whom man's end as seer of God, as contemplator of the eternal, comes into human view; he is also the way to that end. Christ is the one in whom man's subjection to the law is made evident and is realized in perfect obedience; but in him, too, condemnation by the law is made clear; he is thus the figure of tragic manhood; yet he is also the deliverer of man from condemnation, and so man's justifier. Much Protestant ethics thinks of him in this fashion; so it employs the great symbolic figure.

When we think of the Christian ethics as one of responsibility to God in all reactions to action upon us we also are under the neces-

[3] Section heading supplied by editor.

sity of seeing Christ in a double role. For we note that the human problem is this: how can we interpret all actions upon us, especially the decisive action by which we are, and all things are, by which we are destroyed and all things are destroyed, as divine actions, as actions of affirmation and reaffirmation rather than as actions of animosity or of indifference? How is an ethos of universal responsibility possible, even in modest measure, to human beings? That one power is present in all the powers to which we are subject is a presupposition of our lives which we may question intellectually but do not really question in our action. We entertain pluralistic hypotheses about the world in various metaphysical speculations yet we continue to seek to know as those who have a universal intent. We seek a knowledge that will be universally true, though all our propositions are known to be only approximations to universal truth. We have the inconquerable conviction that we confront a oneness behind and in and through all the many-ness in which we live and which we know.

What we cannot believe as personally existent selves is that this One beyond all the many, this power present in all powers, this reason present in all reasons, this idea inclusive of all ideas, this nature behind and through all natures, this environment environing all our environments, is beneficent toward what proceeds from it, or to what it encloses.

But now for Christians Jesus Christ appears not only as the symbol of an ethos in which the ultimate response to the inscrutable power in all things is one of trust. He is also the one who accomplishes in them this strange miracle, that he makes them suspicious of their deep suspicion of the Determiner of Destiny. He turns their reasoning around so that they do not begin with the premise of God's indifference but of his affirmation of the creature, so that the *Gestalt* which they bring to their experiences of suffering as well as of joy, of death as well as of life, is the *Gestalt,* the symbolic form, of

grace. That so to reason and so to perceive requires a great relearn-
ing which is never completed in their lives; that for the most part
they do not reason and interpret on the basis of the new premise but
on that of the old; that they tend to interpret the action upon them
by which they are and by which they cease to be as inimical or indifferent; that they respond therefore for the most part in the manner of an ethics of death, Christians agree. Their true life, man's
true life, is still hidden, hidden, as Paul says, with Christ in God.
That is one of many reasons why they cannot defend themselves or
recommend themselves. But the hope of that life of universal responsibility, of citizenship in the country of being itself, of reaction
in all reactions to the God of grace, to the grace which is God—
that hope is there, and there is rejoicing when the potentiality that
has been put into life becomes for some brief moment an actuality.

That this aspiration and hope has happened in human history and
that it happens in individual life is for the Christian inseparably
connected with Jesus Christ. The hope of glory does enter into
being. When the Christian addresses the Determiner of Destiny
actually, not merely verbally, as Father, he knows he does it in the
name, because of the presence in him, of Jesus Christ. When he
feels and knows himself to be a son of God, an heir in the universe,
at home in the world, he knows this sonship, this at-homeness, as
not only like Jesus Christ's but as actualized by him.

How Jesus Christ in history, and the symbolic Christ within,
reconciles men to God, or God to men, or accomplishes the double
reconciliation of each to each, Christians cannot easily say. Few of
them are satisfied with the theories of the atonement current in the
churches, dependent as these are on questionable images of the
ultimate rightness of God, or of the sources of human estrangement.
To some of us it seems that in the cross of Jesus Christ, in the death
of such a man who trusts God and is responsible to him as a son,
we face the great negative instance or the negation of the premise
that God is love, and that unless this great negative instance—

summarizing and symbolizing all the negative instances—is faced, faith in the universal power as God must rest on quicksand; in facing it, however, we have the demonstration in this very instance of a life-power that is not conquered, not destroyed. Reality maintains and makes powerful such life as this. The ultimate power does manifest itself as the Father of Jesus Christ through his resurrection from death. The resurrection is not manifest to us in physical signs but in his continuing Lordship—his session at the right hand of power, as the old creeds put it. So we apprehend the way of God as manifested not in creation and destruction but in these *and* resurrection, in the raising of the temporal to the eternal plane.

However adequate or inadequate our theories of at-onement or reconciliation may be, the fact remains: the movement beyond resignation to reconciliation is the movement inaugurated and maintained in Christians by Jesus Christ. By Jesus Christ men have been and are empowered to become sons of God—not as those who are saved out of a perishing world but as those who know that the world is being saved. That its being saved from destruction involves the burning up of an infinite amount of tawdry human works, that it involves the healing of a miasmic ocean of disease, the resurrection of the dead, the forgiveness of sins, the making good of an infinite number of irresponsibilities, that such making good is not done except by suffering servants who often do not know the name of Christ though they bear his image—all this Christians know. Nevertheless, they move toward their end and all endings as those who, knowing defeats, do not believe in defeat.

Thus Christians understand themselves and their ethos, or somewhat in this fashion. They cannot boast that they have an excellent way of life for they have little to point to when they boast. They only confess—we were blind in our distrust of being, now we begin to see; we were aliens and alienated in a strange, empty world, now we begin sometimes to feel at home; we were in love with ourselves and all our little cities, now we are falling in love, we think, with being itself, with the city of God, the universal community of which God is the source and governor. And for all this we are indebted to Jesus Christ, in our history, and in that depth of the spirit in which we grope with our theologies and theories of symbols. Could it have so happened otherwise; could the same results have been achieved through other means? Are they being produced elsewhere through other means? That seems possible; nevertheless this one is our physician, this one is our reconciler to the Determiner of our Destiny. To whom else shall we go for words of eternal life, to whom else for the franchise in the universal community?

INDEX

Accountability, theory of responsi-
bility and, 63–65
Action, *see* Response
Agape and Eros (Nygren), 39
Aquinas, Thomas, 10, 26, 49, 128,
134
Aristophanes, 17
Aristotle, 10, 48, 49, 52, 57
Arndt, E. J. F., 11 n.
Art and Illusion (Gombrich), 153 n.
Art forms, symbolism of, 152–153
Auerbach, Erich, 153 n.
Augustine, 21, 26, 30, 39, 128

Barth, Karl, 12, 13, 15, 20, 26, 66,
131, 158
Beach, Waldo, 11 n., 12 n., 19
Bergson, Henri, 99
Bible, *see* Scripture

Biblical Faith and Social Ethics
(Gardner), 12 n.
Bixler, J. S., 11 n.
Bonhoeffer, Dietrich, 12, 13, 20
Broad, C. D., 55
Brunner, Emil, 27, 32
Buber, Martin, 72
Bultmann, Rudolf, 66, 131
Butler, Bishop Joseph, 74

Calhoun, R. L., 11 n.
Calvin, John, 21, 26, 30
Cassirer, Ernst, 151
Christ
redemption through, 174–178
symbolism of, 154–159, 161–178
see also Jesus
Christ and Culture (Niebuhr), 9,
19, 26

179

Christian ethics, *see* Ethics, Christian

Christian Ethics (Beach & Niebuhr), 11 n., 19

Christian Ethos, The (Elert), 15 n.

Church
authority of, 22
purpose of, 11

Church Dogmatics (Barth), 13 n.

Coleridge, S. T., 72 n.

Conscience
selfhood and, 71–79
social theory of, 75–76

Cooley, George Horton, 71

Death
Christ-symbolism and, 154
ethics of, 143, 144, 176
mythology of, 90–107 *passim*

Deontology
moral questions and, 60

Descartes, René, 101, 109

Distrust, *see* Trust

Divine Imperative (Brunner), 27

Edwards, Jonathan, 10, 21, 26

Elert, W., 15 n., 20

Epictetus, 171

Epicureanism, 90–91

Essay concerning Human Understanding, An (Locke), 152 n.

Ethical Relativity (Westermarck), 76 n.

Ethics (Aristotle), 48, 49 n.

Ethics (Bonhoeffer), 12, 13

Ethics, Christian, 159–160
Biblical authority in, 19–25
definition of, 40
egoisms vs. universalisms, 171–172
field of, 10
personal integrity and, 16, 123

Ethics (*Continued*)
personal responsibility, 14–15
responsibility to God, 174–178
scope of, 8–9
self-knowledge and, 15–19
task of, 14
theology of, 7
theory of, 163
typology of, 10
uniqueness of, 14
see also Christ; Death; God; Man; Redeemed; Redemption; Response; Responsibility; Salvation; Self; Selfhood; Self-knowledge; Suffering; Survival

Ethics, Hebrew, 168, 169–170

Ethics, Jewish, 168

Ethics, Stoic, 170–171

Ethics, Zoroastrian, 159

Ethos, Christian, 167–168

Faith
self as interpreter and, 118–119
trust, 118–122

Faith and Ethics, The Theology of H. Richard Niebuhr (Ramsey), 11 n., 26 n.

Fales, W., 57 n.

Feuerbach, Ludwig, 72 n.

Francis (St.), 30

Freedom, 173; self and, 100–106

Frei, Hans, 26 n.

Freud, Sigmund, 75

Fromm, Erich, 36

Gardner, E. Clinton, 12 n.

Gladstone, W. E., 74 n.

God
Christ-symbolism and, 154–159
as Creator, 24, 30–31, 135
as Governor, 31–36
man's response to, 25–41
reconciliation of man to, 43–45

God (*Continued*)
  as Redeemer, 29–30, 36–41
  trinitarian concept of, 24, 27–30
  see also Man; Redeemed; Re-
    demption
Gombrich, E. H. J., 153 n.
Gospel, the Church and the World,
  The (Latourette), 11 n.
Gustafson, James, 12 n.

Hamartia, 16, 131
Hartmann, Nicolai, 91
Hartt, Julian, 12 n.
Heidegger, Martin, 112, 116
Heim, Karl, 112
Heritage of the Reformation, The
  (Arndt), 11 n.
History
  self in, 98–107
  symbol and, 156–157
Homo dialogicus, 160
Homo faber, 160
Homo politicus, 160
Hugo, Victor, 92
Hume, David, 75

Ideals of East and West, The (Saunders), 117 n.
Integrity, *see* Self
Interpretation, theory of responsibility and, 63, 101–107, 117–
  118
Isaiah, 67, 169, 173

Jaspers, Karl, 112
Jesus, ethos of, 167, 168; *see also*
  Christ

Kant, Immanuel, 74, 75, 91, 92
Kant's Critique of Practical Reason
  and Other Works on the The-
  ory of Ethics, 74 n., 92 n.
Kierkegaard, Søren, 92, 121

Language as symbolic system, 152
Latourette, K. S., 11 n.
Law, *see under* Man
Life
  Christ-symbolism, 154–159, 162
  ethics of, 143
  interpretation of, through sym-
    bolic forms, 149–160
  moral life as responsible life, 65
  purposiveness of, 60
  of responsibility, 89
  see also Ethics, Christian; God;
    Man; Response; Responsibility;
    Salvation; Self; Selfhood; Self-
    knowledge; Suffering
Lippmann, Walter, 17
Locke, John, 152
Love, meaning of, 11
Luther, Martin, 21, 26, 27, 39, 118

Man
  as image-user, 151–154
  man-the-answerer, 56–60
  man-the-citizen, 51–54, 92
  man-the-maker, 48–51, 69, 70, 88,
    90, 91, 108, 131, 133, 135, 136
  man-under-law, 128–135
  as self-legislator, 54, 70–71, 88
  as symbolic animal, 161
  see also God; Self; Selfhood; Self-
    knowledge
Marcel, Gabriel, 112
Maurice, F. D., 14, 21, 27, 37
Mead, G. H., 10, 71, 72, 76
Meaning of Revelation, The (Nie-
  buhr), 11, 14, 25, 37 n.
Metanoia, 143–144
Mimesis (Auerbach), 153 n.
Moral life, *see* Life
Moral philosophy, *see* Philosophy
Morals of the Catholic Church, The
  (Augustine), 39
Murray, Gilbert, 90

Nature of Religious Experience, The (Bixler, *et al.*), 11 n.
Niebuhr, H. R., 11 n.
Nygren, Anders, 39

Obiter Scripta (Buchler & Schwartz), 114 n.
Oxford English Dictionary, 47 n.

Pacifism, Christian, 36 n.
Paul, 21, 39, 127, 156, 176
Pepper, Stephen, 153 n.
Philosophy
 terminology, 42, 45–46
 see also Ethics; Life; Responsibility
Philosophy of the Present, The (Mead), 77 n.
Piper, Otto, 20
Plato, 99
Preface to Morals, A (Lippmann), 17
Purpose of the Church and Its Ministry (Niebuhr), 10

Radical Monotheism and Western Culture (Niebuhr), 10, 22, 25
Ramsey, Paul, 11 n., 12 n.
Redeemed
 ethics of the, 38
 life of the, 130
 see also Redemption; Salvation
Redemption, 142–144
 ethics of, 36–40
 through Christ, 174–178
 see also Redeemed; Salvation
Religion within the Limits of Reason Alone (Kant), 92 n.
Response, 136–145
 action as, 16–17, 61–68
 ethics of (Stoic). 170
 to God, 25–41
 to natural events, 102

Response (*Continued*)
 to others, 100–107, 116
 theory of responsibility and, 61–62
 time and, 98
 see also Ethics, Christian; Life; Man; Responsibility; Self; Selfhood; Self-knowledge
Responsibility
 decision and, 60
 Christ-symbolism and, 161–178
 elements in symbol of, 47–68
 ethics of, 167–178
 pattern of, 65
 society and, 69–89
 symbolism of, 56–68
 theory of, 61–68
 usage of term, 47–48
 see also Ethics, Christian; Faith; Freedom; History; Interpretation; Life; Man; Salvation; Self; Selfhood; Self-knowledge Sin; Time
Ritschl, ethics of, 174
Rousseau, J. J., 128
Royce, Josiah, 83

Salvation, 133, 135–145; *see also* Redeemed; Redemption
Santayana, George, 113, 114 n.
Saunders, K., 117 n.
Schrader, George, 12 n.
Scripture, authority of, 22–25
Self
 destruction of, 114–115, 132
 integrity of, 16, 123
 as interpreting agent, 109–126
 response-analysis, 136–145
 self-consciousness, 117
 unity of, 125
 see also History; Selfhood; Self-knowledge; Time

Selfhood
  acountability and, 82–89
  conscience and, 71–79
  man's condition in, 137
  mature, 83
  and response to natural events, 79–84
  social nature of, 71 ff.
  see also History; Self; Self-knowledge; Time
Self-knowledge, 15–19
  human condition and, 133
  images employed toward, 48–60
  responsibility and, 69–79
  see also Self; Selfhood
Seneca, 171
Sin, self and, 131–145
Smith, Adam, 75, 76
Social Psychology of George Herbert Mead (Strauss), 72 n.
Social solidarity, theory of responsibility and, 65
Social Sources of Denominationalism, The (Niebuhr), 1
Society, see Responsibility; Selfhood
Socrates, 15, 52
Spinoza, 26, 34, 58, 113, 128, 171
Strauss, A., 72 n.
Studdert-Kennedy, G. A., 155

Suffering, ethics of, 58–60
Sullivan, Harry Stack, 71
Summa Theologica (Aquinas), 49 n.
Survival, ethics of, 99–100
Symbol
  necessity for, 157
  see also Art forms; Christ; History; Language; Life; Man; Responsibility; Symbolism
Symbolism, Christian, 149–160

Theologische Ethik (Thielicke), 20 n.
Theology, definition of, 40
Thielicke, Helmut, 20
Tillich, Paul, 26
Time, self in, 90–97
Tolstoy, Leo, 34
Tractatus de intellectus emendatione (Spinoza), 58 n.
Trust and distrust, 118–122, 144
Two Sources of Morality and Religion, The (Bergson), 99

Wesley, John, 21
Westermarck, Edward, 75, 76
Wisdom and Responsibility (Fales), 57 n.
Woolman, John, 30
World Hypotheses (Pepper), 153 n.

Printed in the United States
72874LV00005B/202-240